CÉSAR CHÁVEZ
Fighting for Migrant Farmworkers

REBELS WITH A CAUSE

CÉSAR CHÁVEZ
Fighting for Migrant Farmworkers

Kathlyn Gay

Enslow Publishing
101 W. 23rd Street
Suite 240
New York, NY 10011
USA

enslow.com

Published in 2018 by Enslow Publishing, LLC.
101 W. 23rd Street, Suite 240, New York, NY 10011

Copyright © 2018 by Enslow Publishing, LLC.

All rights reserved.

No part of this book may be reproduced by any means without the written permission of the publisher.

Library of Congress Cataloging-in-Publication Data

Names: Gay, Kathlyn, author.
Title: César Chávez: fighting for migrant farmworkers/ Kathlyn Gay.
Description: New York : Enslow Publishing, 2018. | Series: Rebels with a cause | Includes bibliographical references and index. | Audience: Grades 7-12. Identifiers: LCCN 2016057508 | ISBN 9780766089518 (library bound : alk. paper) Subjects: LCSH: Chávez, César, 1927-1993–Juvenile literature. | United Farm Workers—History—Juvenile literature. | Labor leaders—United States–Biography—Juvenile literature. | Mexican American migrant agricultural laborers—Biography—Juvenile literature. | Agricultural laborers—Labor unions—United States—History—Juvenile literature. Classification: LCC HD6509.C48 G38 2018 | DDC 331.88/13092 [B]—dc23 LC record available at https://lccn.loc.gov/2016057508

Printed in the United States of America

To Our Readers: We have done our best to make sure all website addresses in this book were active and appropriate when we went to press. However, the author and the publisher have no control over and assume no liability for the material available on those websites or on any websites they may link to. Any comments or suggestions can be sent by email to customerservice@enslow.com.

Photo Credits: Cover, p. 3 Patrick Grehan/Corbis/Getty Images; p. 7 John W. Keith/Archive Photos/Getty Images; p. 9 Icon Communications/Archive Photos/Getty Images; pp. 12, 14–15, 26–27, 46–47, 54–55 Cathy Murphy/Hulton Archive/Getty Images; pp. 19, 21, 43, 91 © 1976 George Ballis/Take Stock/The Image Works; p. 23 Central Press/Hulton Archive/Getty Images; p. 31 Photofusion/Universal Images Group/Getty Images; p. 37 Keystone-France/Gamma-Keystone/Getty Images; p. 40 Arthur Schatz/The LIFE Picture Collection/Getty Images; pp. 51, 85, 100–101 © AP Images; pp. 58–59 Bettmann/Getty Images; p. 63 ANDREW HOLBROOKE/Corbis/Getty Images; p. 69 Richard Thornton/Shutterstock.com;
p. 74 Bill Eppridge/The LIFE Picture Collection/Getty Images; p. 77 Terry Fincher/Hulton Archive/Getty Images; p. 82 Grey Villet/The LIFE Picture Collection/Getty Images; p. 87 U.S. Department of Labor; p. 94 Geoff Hansen/Hulton Archive/Getty Images; p. 97 Mike Nelson/AFP/Getty Images; interior pages borders, pp. 6–7 background Eky Studio/Shutterstock.com.

Contents

Introduction 6
1 **Overcoming Hard Times** 9
2 **Community Organizing** 21
3 **Farmworkers Organize** 36
4 **Pressing On** 50
5 **No Rest for Strikers** 62
6 **"Lett-us" Strike Again** 73
7 **Internal and External Scuffles** 84
8 **A Downward Trend and Tributes** 93

Conclusion 102
Chronology 105
Chapter Notes 107
Glossary 117
Further Reading 119
Index 121

INTRODUCTION

During the 1950s and 1960s, campains to improve the condition of migrant farmworkers, such as César Chávez and his large extended family, had to vie with other major issues provoking marches, sit-ins, rallies, and other public protests. The civil rights movement was well underway. Thousands of marchers, boycotters, and other protesters increased their crusades to abolish discrimination against African Americans and to demand voting rights. Martin Luther King Jr. became a prominent leader and was murdered for his efforts. And African American protesters were met with violent resistance from Ku Klux Klan members, white supremacists, and other segregationists. Riots, bombings, beatings, and shootings were common.

During the 1950s anticommunist fever rose to a fever pitch in the United States. It was a "cold war" (nonmilitary combat) against the Soviet Union and its communist government. US senator Joseph McCarthy led an infamous campaign, claiming that communists were everywhere in the federal government and military. He

Introduction

Many farmworkers took their families into the fields to work, such as this family harvesting onions in California in the 1950s.

lied about and ruined the lives of many loyal US citizens with his false accusations.

Through the 1960s, small groups (primarily students) and national organizations demanded an end to American involvement in the Vietnam War. Others supported US military efforts to protect South Vietnam from the communist North Vietnamese National Liberation Front, also known as the Vietcong. The rationale for the war was to prevent what was called the "domino effect"—one Asian country after another falling to a communist takeover.

Along with anti-Vietnam and civil rights protests, the nation was **pummeled with women's demands for equal educational, employment opportunities, and pay.** Pro-life and pro-choice abortion controversies erupted in numerous cities nationwide. Native Americans organized to protect their lands and preserve their cultures and tribal self-government. Homosexuals, who had organized in earlier decades, made increasing public calls to end legal discrimination based on sexual orientation. **Americans of Mexican heritage battled for job opportunities and political power while facing discriminatory practices because of the color of their skin, their culture, and their native language.**

During these decades of social upheaval, César Chávez began his efforts to unite migratory farmworkers. It was a formidable task but a cause to which he was deeply committed. Yet, nothing in his first few years of life indicated that he would become a highly respected, even revered, leader of a Mexican American union. He would also become a controversial figure, a rebel dedicated to a cause that had spiritual as well as practical underpinnings.

1

Overcoming Hard Times

It was late October 1929, and for two days newspapers across the United States announced in huge headlines "Black Tuesday," "The Day America Crashed," and "Wall Street Crash!" The stock market had fallen, banks had closed, and people across the United States lost bil-

The stock market crash in 1929 led to panic across the United States, and newspapers carried headlines like this.

lions of dollars in investments. It was the beginning of the Great Depression, which would last well into the 1930s.

Millions of Americans suffered economic catastrophes. They lost jobs, savings, homes, and properties; they became impoverished. Some panicked and committed suicide by jumping from tall buildings and leaping from bridges.

Imagine, during all this, a little boy in his toddler overalls playing in front of his desert home, laughing and chasing his older sister. He is too young to know anything about banks and investments in stock markets or, for that matter, anything at all about buying and selling. He is two years old and has no inkling that soon his family will face dire circumstances. The little boy, César Estrada Chávez, does not yet understand his family is among those who will experience hardship.

As the Depression began, César's parents, Librado and Juana, were struggling to make a living, but they managed to keep their family fed, clothed, and cared for in a secure adobe home. They lived on desert land near Yuma, Arizona, about a mile from the California border. The acreage had originally been homesteaded in the late 1800s by César's grandfather Césario Chávez, who fled Chihuahua, Mexico, to find a better life in the United States for his family. Years later, Césario's son Librado purchased the property, which included several buildings and livestock. He also operated a general store and postal service on the homestead.

Chávez's Birth

Named after his grandfather, César Chávez was born on March 31, 1927. He was the couple's second child and the oldest son. He recalled in later years that he had a happy childhood and loving parents. César's father was often too busy to be with his children but was affectionate when around them. He taught his children to work hard and to be respectful of others, especially those less fortunate.

César's mother was the one who kept the family together. She was a strict disciplinarian and insisted that her children do their chores and their schoolwork. Although there was no church close by, she and César's grandmother, Mama Tella, as she was called, taught César and his siblings their Catholic prayers. "Chávez's mother helped shape his beliefs about nonviolence and morality. She spent a great deal of time with her four children telling them many *cuentos* (stories), *consejos* (advice), and *dichos* (sayings), all of which had a moral point," according to Richard Griswold del Castillo, a Chávez biographer.[1]

Every morning, Mama Tella required César and his sister to say the rosary with her. She drilled them on the catechism—the teachings of the Catholic Church. She "prepared César and his older sister Rita so well for their first communion that the children were able to respond to the catechism questions accurately enough to convince a skeptical parish priest that they were able to receive the sacrament," wrote Fredrick Dalton in his book *The Moral Vision of César Chávez*.[2]

Disaster

When Librado purchased the Chávez homestead, he needed to borrow nearly $3,000 to pay his mortgage. According to biographer Miriam Pawel, Librado liked to

César's parents attend a rally to organize farmworkers.

gamble and was often absent from his varied businesses. He was unable to pay taxes on the land or repay the loan. His debts increased. By 1929, when César was just two years old, the bank foreclosed on his family's property and auctioned the homestead, selling it to the bank president for $1,750.[3] The family stayed on until they could gather a few belongings and find a place to live.

"Oh, I remember having to move out of our house," César recalled years later. "My father had brought in a team of horses and wagon. We had always lived in that house, and we couldn't understand why we were moving out." He added:

> We had been poor, but we knew every night there was a bed there, and that this was our room. There was a

kitchen. It was sort of a settled life, and we had chickens and hogs, eggs and all those things. But that all of a sudden changed. When you're small, you can't figure these things out. You know something's not right and you don't like it, but you don't question it and you don't let that get you down. You sort of just continue to move.[4]

Not only did the César's family lose their homestead and most of their belongings, they faced unemployment. In the midst of the Great Depression, there were few available jobs. In addition, severe droughts had wiped out crops. The Chávezes had little choice except to join the 200,000 to 350,000 migrant workers who followed crops, planting, cultivating, and harvesting them throughout the United States. They headed for California.

> "We had always lived in that house, and we couldn't understand why we were moving out."

Migrant Life

As César was growing up, his migrant family worked according to seasonal harvests. They picked peas and lettuce in the winter, cherries and beans in the spring, corn and grapes in the summer, and cotton in the fall. César and his family "worked in…Brawley, Oxnard, Atascadero, Gonzales, King City, Salinas, McFarland, Delano, Wasco, Selma, Kingsburg, and Mendota."[5] Like other migrant workers, the Chávez family toiled long, grueling days for little pay—sometimes even cheated out of those meager wages. Workers had no recourse; few laws existed for protection. In short, migrant workers were powerless.

THE SHORT-HANDLED HOE

One of the agricultural tools used by migrant workers throughout much of the twentieth century was the short-handled hoe, or *el cortito*, which looked like a

Overcoming Hard Times

regular gardening hoe. The handle was very short, and migrants had to use it to cultivate fields. They had to stay in a stooped position during their twelve-hour days as they moved along to weed or thin out crops like sugar beets. If they stood up, supervisors yelled at them to get back to work. It was debilitating, and many workers suffered spinal damage while working with this tool. Use of the hoe for migrant fieldwork was outlawed in 1975.

Migrant farmworkers labored long, back-breaking hours in agricultural fields like this.

According to Richard Griswold del Castillo of San Diego State University:

> *In Oxnard, the Chávez family was homeless and had to spend the winter living in a tent that was soggy from either rain or fog. They used a 50-gallon (189-liter) can for a stove and tried to keep wood dry inside the tent. The children did odd jobs around town while the adults tried to find work. Moving north to the San Joaquin Valley, they stayed in labor camps where they lived in tiny tarpaper-and-wood cabins without indoor plumbing and with a single electric light. There were no paved streets, and in the winter the ground turned into a slippery quagmire.*[6]

Facing Discrimination

Discrimination in the state was overt and common in the late 1930s. There were "White Trade Only" or "No Dogs or Mexicans Allowed" signs throughout the Southwest during César's youth. When the family returned to Yuma, Arizona, for a short time, they faced the same kind of racism. Wherever the Chávez family worked and lived, they encountered prejudice. "Everywhere we went, to school, to church, to the movies there was an attack on our culture and our language, an attempt to make us conform to the 'American Way,'" as César recalled much later.[7]

Because the Chávez family moved so often, César attended numerous schools, all of which he disliked, although he made good grades in reading and arithmetic. Most teachers were Anglos (primarily white English-speaking people) and often held racist views of Mexican Americans, especially those who spoke Spanish in class or on the playground. Spanish was forbidden in school, and kids were punished—usually slapped on the hand with a ruler or insulted in some way—if they broke the rule. By the time he reached eighth grade, César was disgusted with his schooling, which had nothing to do with his way of life. He quit his formal education in 1942 and became a migrant farm worker. It was a choice also prompted by the fact that his father could no longer work because of a car accident and César did not want his mother to do manual labor in the fields. And he was well aware that supervisors and other workers often hassled girls and women, making sexual comments and advances. So he took his father's place as a migrant worker.

Many migrant workers faced health and safety hazards on the job. They worked without adequate toilets, drinking water, and hand-washing facilities in the fields. Without sufficient drinking water, workers become dehydrated or suffered from other heat-related problems. Indeed, César's father was disabled for a time because of heat stroke. In addition, migrant workers frequently were (and still are) exposed to toxic pesticides while planting or harvesting in the fields. No one knows the exact number of poisonings because victims may not seek medical care; they seldom have health insurance coverage and are reluctant to miss work. If farmworkers were able to get to a health center, doctors might fail to diagnose accurately because poisoning symptoms are similar to those associated with the flu.

Military Service and Marriage

In 1946, after World War II ended, César Chávez joined the US Navy. In some Chávez biographies, his enlistment date is reported as 1944. But Chávez backdated his enrollment on some occasions, "claiming he signed up in 1944 rather than in 1946, a small change reflecting his calculation that [being a] war veteran would prove a useful embellishment."[8] Before enlisting, he had been thinning sugar beets with his father, and he was eager to get away from this back-breaking labor. Neither of his parents approved, but he enlisted anyway for two years.

After he began his service, Chávez quickly became disgruntled. He noted that his two years in the navy were the "worst of [his] life." He hated the regimentation and being treated "like a piece of equipment." Like other Mexican Americans on his ship, he was a deckhand. "Most of my duty was in small boats," he explained. "I was also on a crew transport that went to the Marinara Islands, but I was never in combat."[9]

Chávez was honorably discharged in 1948. He wanted to take advantage of veteran benefits to further his education. But he had not graduated from high school, so he only qualified for vocational training. He was not interested in such training and decided to return to Delano, California. There he reconnected with Helen Fabela, who lived in Delano. The two had met earlier, before Chávez enlisted, and they soon began dating. Within a short time, Fabela was pregnant, and in October 1948, the couple traveled to Reno, Nevada, to marry in a civil court. After a brief honeymoon, they returned to Delano to live. Their son, Fernando, was

César Chávez and his wife, Helen, lead a march together in 1966.

born in February 1949. Eventually, they would have eight children.[10]

In 1949, César and Helen moved to San Jose, California, to be with the extended Chávez family, settling in a San Jose barrio called Sal Si Puedes—meaning "Escape if You Can." It was a place where many Mexican farmworkers lived in "shabby shacks and old houses with outside privies in the back. There were of course no sewers. Each lot was crowded with houses and surrounded by tall, unpainted fences," Chávez recalled in his autobiography.[11] His family had endured even worse conditions as migrants, sometimes living in cars or trucks, tents, barns, horse stables, or garages, or if housing was provided, metal shacks with no plumbing or electricity.

While in San Jose, Chávez worked in lumberyards for a time stacking wood. Then the couple returned to Delano. Chávez had earned enough at the lumberyards to buy a small house and settle in with his family. In Delano, he would learn about ways to overcome oppression and to serve the community.

2
Community Organizing

The Chávez home in Sal Si Puedes was often a center for visiting neighbors and extended family members and coworkers. But it was unusual for strangers to stop by—especially unknown Anglos. So it was quite unexpected when first an Irish Catholic priest

Chávez presents a sign that will be used when picketing grape fields in California.

and later a community organizer visited the Chávezes in the early 1950s. They had a profound effect on both César and Helen.

An Influential Priest

Over the years, César Chávez had had little to do with the Roman Catholic Church, even though his mother, who was devout, encouraged her children to observe religious teachings. But in the early 1950s, a priest, Father Donald McDonnell, held outdoor meetings in the barrio. McDonnell also set up a small church in a shack near the Chávez home. The building, which was also used as a health clinic, was so dilapidated that during the Christmas season the roof leaked and flooded the nativity scene.

César and Helen attended McDonnell's church and discovered that the priest empathized with the plight of people in the barrio and the injustices farmworkers suffered. McDonnell had been a pastor in Northern California, where he ministered to poor Mexican American farmers and campaigned for social justice. He spoke numerous languages, including Chinese, Japanese, Portuguese, and Spanish. Wherever his ministry, he delivered his message of social justice in the native language of the population. The priest explained Catholic teachings and emphasized the rights and dignity of workers. He insisted that people should organize to confirm their rights.

When talking with the Chávezes, McDonnell explained how the church could help in the struggle for social change and the right to organize labor unions. Since Chávez enjoyed reading, the priest gave Chávez books about Mohandas Gandhi, who

Gandhi, leader of the independence movement in India, believed in and practiced nonviolent civil disobedience in the 1930s to free India from British rule.

believed in nonviolent resistance and initiated an act of civil disobedience in 1930 when the government of India placed a tax on salt. Gandhi led a march of 200 miles (322 kilometers) to the sea, where he and his devoted followers evaporated seawater to make salt. McDonnell also shared papers by two Catholic popes who encouraged workers to unify. In addition, Chávez read several biographies of St. Francis of Assisi, a Roman Catholic friar who lived in poverty, despite being born into wealth, and dedicated his life to helping the downtrodden. Chávez's reading, along with McDonnell's nurturing, laid a foundation for later commitments to organize migrant workers.

The Model Organizer

Another Anglo who made a major difference in Chávez's life was Fred Ross Sr., a tall, middle-aged man. Beginning in the late 1930s, Ross had worked with neighborhood, civic, and religious groups to fight discrimination and social injustice. For example, after World War II, according to scholar Peter Dreier, "Ross spearheaded eight Civic Unity Leagues in California's conservative Citrus Belt, bringing Mexican Americans and African Americans together to battle segregation in schools, skating rinks and movie theaters." Dreier added:

> *In the 1950s, Ross worked in the Latino barrios of Los Angeles, San Jose, and other cities to build chapters of the Community Service Organization (CSO), a civil rights and civic improvement group, in California and Arizona. The founding leaders of the CSO included members of the steelworkers, clothing*

Community Organizing

CIVIL DISOBEDIENCE

Civil disobedience has a long history both in the US and worldwide. The term "civil disobedience" was the title of an essay by Henry David Thoreau (1817–1862) of Massachusetts. Thoreau publicly protested the US invasion of Mexico in 1846; he believed the conflict was a US effort to occupy the territory and expand slavery in the Southwest. In defiance, Thoreau refused to pay a local tax, so the tax collector ordered a sheriff to arrest Thoreau. But an unknown person paid the tax, and Thoreau was released. He then gave a lecture, which he published in 1849 with the title "Civil Disobedience."

Since Thoreau's time, countless activists have practiced civil disobedience. They have disobeyed laws to protest slavery, war, environmental destruction, prison brutality, government policies, discrimination, and many other causes. Civil disobedience practitioners risk being harassed, physically attacked, jailed, or even murdered for their actions.

workers, meat cutters, and other unions. They formed the core of CSO's early leadership who built a powerful coalition that included the NAACP [National Association for the Advancement of Colored People], the Japanese American Citizens League, the Catholic

César Chávez: Fighting for Migrant Farmworkers

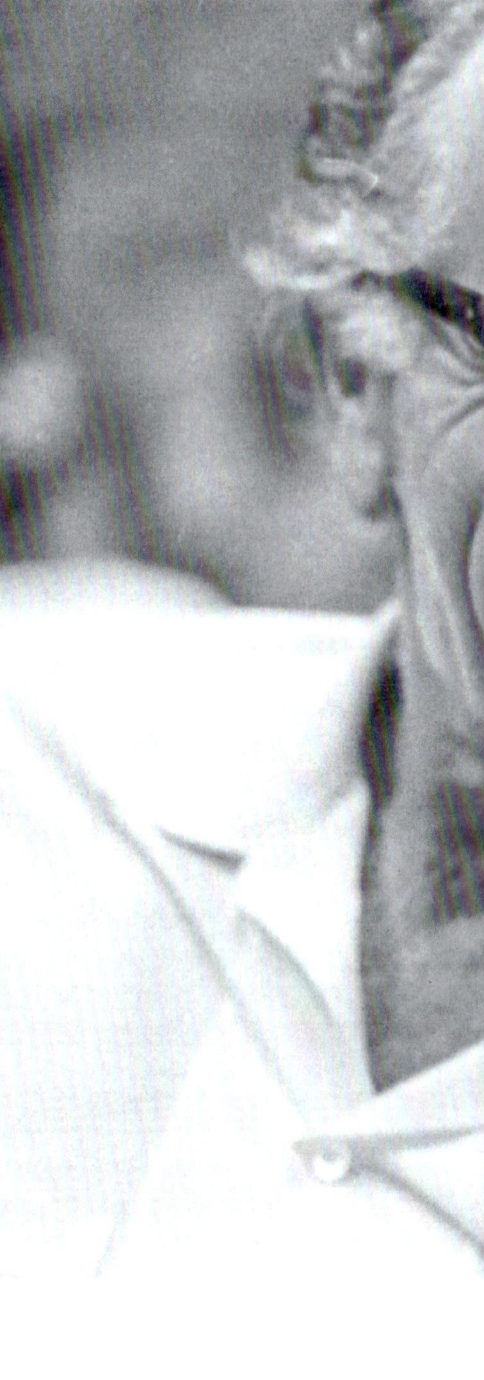

Church, and the Jewish community. Together they fought for fair housing, employment and working conditions.[1]

At the urging of Father McDonnell, Ross decided to knock on the door of the Chávez home. César Chávez was leery. Was this gringo some kind of social worker, or maybe a curious researcher wanting to find out how people in a barrio live? Chávez was somewhat prickly, and he could get angry—he had a temper when riled. But he welcomed Ross into his humble home.

Ross soon explained his mission, and Chávez listened carefully—one of his positive characteristics. The tall Anglo had come to recruit Chávez, to ask him to join the Community Service Organization (CSO), which Ross founded in 1947. Ross told Chávez about CSO and what the organization had been doing:

Community Organizing

Fred Ross Sr. and Chávez huddle to plan strategies for organizing farmworkers.

- Operating a federal labor camp near Bakersfield, California, where migrant farmworkers from Oklahoma (disparagingly called "Okies) were located;
- Helping Japanese Americans return to their homes and get jobs after they were released from concentration camps where they had been forced to live during World War II;
- Urging Mexican Americans to become politically active, and to register to vote; and
- Organizing minority parents to help end school segregation in California.

As Ross talked, Chávez became interested and wanted to hear more. So did Helen. Chávez recalled much later: "Fred did such a good job of explaining how poor people could build power that I could even taste it. I thought, gee, it's like digging a hole. There's nothing complicated about it."[2]

> "Fred [Ross] did such a good job of explaining how poor people could build power that I could even taste it."

Joining and Working for CSO

During Ross's visit, Chávez began asking questions about how CSO could help farmworkers. Ross assured Chávez that once the organization became strong, they could create a labor union. That convinced Chávez, and he signed on in 1952. He soon learned, though, that organizing wasn't as easy as "digging a hole."

To support his growing family, Chávez had to keep working as a farm laborer. He picked fruit during the day and in the evening talked to other workers, convincing them to register to vote. Within two months, he had registered more than two thousand people. He also led campaigns to end racial and ethnic discrimination in schools and workplaces. He was so enthusiastic and so committed that he neglected his work and lost his job. He collected unemployment and when that ran out, Helen went to work for ten hours a day at a job she hated—thinning onion plants in the fields. The Chávez's son Fernando also went to work, earning $1.00 an hour picking grapes.[3]

Ross offered Chávez a full-time position as a CSO organizer. With Father McDonnell's encouragement, Chávez accepted. He recruited people of Mexican heritage in their homes, at meetings, on the street, and in the CSO office, encouraging them to join CSO and to work for political empowerment by registering to vote. He had a patient, methodical approach: talking and listening to individuals one at a time, staying with them for hours if necessary, going from one house and then another, block after block until he had built a coalition. He also held group meetings. Although César was hesitant to be a public speaker, he discovered that he could hold people's attention at organized gatherings.

Nevertheless, it was not easy to convince people to unify and fight for their rights. Such action could cost them their livelihoods or even their homes, and in some cases threatened their very existence.

Chávez continued his work with Ross and the CSO, registering thousands of Mexican American voters. As a result, a political confrontation developed. Republican leadership feared that Mexican Americans would register as Democrats and form a powerful political bloc. "Republicans decided to challenge first-time Mexican American voters at the polls," according to Richard Griswold del Castillo. "Chávez signed a letter addressed to the State Attorney General protesting the Republican intimidation tactics. In return, the Republicans began to accuse Chávez of being a communist. FBI agents were summoned to interview him, and stories appeared in the local newspaper implying that he had been influenced by communists."[4] But César's supporters, particularly church

COMMUNISM: THE "RED SCARE"

The threat of communism—often described as the "Red Scare" because of communism's red flag—had an enormous impact on American politics in the 1940s and 1950s. "In response to allegations that communists had infiltrated the State Relief Administration, the California State Legislature began in 1940 what was to become a thirty-one-year investigation into un-American activities in California," according to the California Office of

Community Organizing

During the 1950s, Chávez was investigated for communist activities although he was not a communist.

Secretary of State. "Various committees produced or received thousands of documents, audiotapes, [and] approximately 125,000 index cards tracking an estimated 20,000 individuals or organizations." There were also reports on César Chávez and his organizing activities.[5]

leaders, publicly vouched for him and showed there was no evidence of communist sympathies.

Struggles and Turmoil

The decade of the 1950s was a time of turmoil for Mexican Americans and other minorities. Struggles for civil rights of African Americans were often met with violence. Native Americans, immigrants of Asian descent, and people of color in general faced discrimination in schools, in the workplace, in businesses, and in political power.

The US government created a program using the racial epithet "Operation Wetback" to deport large numbers of illegal Mexican immigrants who worked as farm laborers. President Dwight D. Eisenhower initiated the program in 1954. "The Eisenhower mass deportation policy was tragic," Alfonso Aguilar of the American Principles Project's Latino Partnership recalled in a 2015 interview. "Human rights were violated. People were removed to distant locations without food and water. There were many deaths, unnecessary deaths. Sometimes even US citizens of Hispanic origin, of Mexican origin were removed. It was a travesty."[6]

Before the infamous "wetback" program there was another US government effort that attacked immigrant farmworkers. During World War II, many American citizens of Mexican lineage left migratory farm labor for jobs in industry or they joined the armed forces. Nearly 400,000 Mexican Americans served in the military during the war. With so many migrants leaving farm labor, the need for workers increased dramatically. As a result, the US government, by executive order, established the Bracero Program in 1942.

Officially named the Mexican Farm Labor Program, it was a bilateral agreement between the governments of Mexico and the United States. The agreement allowed "millions of Mexican men to come to the United States to work on, short-term, primarily agricultural labor contracts." However, the program continued for more than two decades with "4.6 million contracts … signed, with many individuals returning several times on different contracts, making it the largest US contract labor program," according to the Center for History and the New Media.

The program was controversial from the beginning. Farmers welcomed *braceros* (manual laborers) but labor unions did not, which led to "animosity and discrimination against Mexicans and Mexican Americans alike," the center noted. "Mexican nationals, desperate for work, were willing to take arduous jobs at wages scorned by most Americans. Farmworkers already living in the United States worried that braceros would compete for jobs and lower wages." In short, Mexican and native workers suffered while growers benefited from plentiful, cheap labor. [7]

Chávez in Charge

After he was hired by the CSO, Chávez worked tirelessly for the organization. He traveled throughout California establishing service centers in diverse areas; he was on the road more often than being home. His voter registration drives were so successful that Ross promoted him. Chávez became a statewide director and earned $58 per week, up from his former $35 weekly pay. Ross sent him to cities and towns like Bakersfield, Hanford, Madera, Salinas, and

Visalia, which meant that he and his family had to move every few months.

Ross and Chávez were able to set up CSO chapters, but after they left an area, the organizations slowly collapsed. Chávez frequently had to return to reinvigorate and reestablish chapters. It was grueling work. Chávez often spent twelve to fourteen hours a day on the job. At a later time, speaking to a group of civil rights workers, he explained:

> *In community organizing you need continuous program that meets the needs of the people in the organization. I have seen many groups attempt community organization and many have failed. The biggest reason for this is that there is a big emphasis on meetings and discussion and writing up programs and not on working with the people. Many organizers get lost in the shuffle of going to meetings, and somehow those who are being organized are lost.*[8]

In spite of his successes, Chávez was unable to concentrate his efforts on farmworkers, which he had long hoped to do. The CSO was focused primarily on organizing Mexican Americans in small towns and cities. But in 1958, CSO sent Chávez to Oxnard, California, where lemon workers were on strike. The labor union feared that braceros were taking away jobs from local farmworkers. Chávez helped reveal the facts in the situation: under the Bracero Program no braceros were allowed to replace local workers; braceros could be hired only if there was a legitimate labor shortage. Chávez "found a corrupt system that was controlled by the growers in league with state and federal officials. The growers falsely claimed the existence of labor shortages, then exploited the braceros by recruiting many more than were needed, giving them only occasional work at lower pay while charging them inflated prices for room and board," according to del Castillo.[9]

Chávez worked with the labor union to protest, picket, march, boycott, and lobby to get rid of corrupt government officials. The campaign was a success, which led to another promotion for Chávez. He became national director of the CSO in 1958, and that meant moving to Los Angeles, the organization's headquarters. César continued his almost nonstop organizing, while Helen worked in orchards picking fruit to earn income for their family. Along with her husband, Helen hoped that soon the CSO would work with farm laborers. But that turned out to be futile hope, and César decided he had to make a change.

3
Farmworkers Organize

Chávez's frustration with the CSO increased. Although by the early 1960s chapters were successful, they were no longer focused on poor farmworkers. Chávez complained that many chapter leaders were middle class and often better educated than the workers who needed representation. These leaders could not empathize with or understand the needs of laborers struggling for survival. As an example, Chávez noted that some CSO leaders opted to meet with politicians in expensive hotel conference rooms, which supposedly would be a more respectable place than, say, a housing project meeting room. Chávez reluctantly went along with that supposition at first, but years later he said, "I was naïve enough in the beginning to buy that."[1] He insisted that the CSO should meet in a facility accessible to poor farmworkers.

Another factor was troubling Chávez. He held a firm commitment to be a "servant of the people," to empower farmworkers by nonviolent means, following the teachings of Gandhi and of Saint Francis. He believed in sacrifice, sometimes to the detriment of his family by refusing a pay raise and spending countless hours away from home. Chávez was constantly helping needy people with such tasks as filling out forms to apply for citizenship and

Mexican workers labor in Texas fields during the 1950s.

getting medical and food assistance. Addressing a group many years later, Chávez noted:

> *All my life, I have been driven by one dream, one goal, one vision: To overthrow a farm labor system in this nation which treats farm workers as if they were…beasts of burden—to be used and discarded… My motivation comes from my personal life—from watching what my mother and father went through when I was growing up; from what we experienced as migrant farm workers in California. That dream, that vision, grew from my own experience with racism…with the desire to be treated fairly and to see my people treated as human beings and not as chattel. It grew from anger and rage…when people of my color were denied the right to see a movie or eat at a restaurant in many parts of California. It grew from the frustration and humiliation…In San Jose, in Los Angeles and in other urban communities, we—the Mexican American people—were dominated by a majority that was Anglo…[T]he only answer—the only hope—was in organizing. More of us had to become citizens. We had to register to vote. And people like me had to develop the skills it would take to organize.*[2]

"You must become a servant of the people. When you do, you can demand their commitment in return."

In 1962, Chávez made a major and difficult decision. He resigned from the CSO and left Los Angeles. He and his family moved back to Delano, California, where César and Helen had first met. César chose Delano because his brother, Richard, and Helen's sisters lived there. He knew that if he found no source of income at least the extended family would provide meals.

After the Chávezes moved into a small house, César took the family on a weeklong vacation—a rare event. César, Helen, and their eight children camped in a state park near Oxnard. No doubt, Helen greatly appreciated the vacation. She was the one who bore the brunt of César's constant absences and near-obsessive devotion to his cause. But she went along willingly because she too believed in campaigning for farmworkers.

Planning and Preparing

Delano, California, is in the southern part of the San Joaquin Valley, the state's top agricultural region and a major source of the nation's supply of produce. A great variety of fruits and vegetables grow in its fertile soil. César knew the area well and began planning how he would organize farmworkers. First, he read whatever he could find about unions. He knew it was necessary to form a union—an organized group of workers who together could use their strength to have a voice in their working conditions. Chávez talked to people about past attempts to form unions that had been failures or resulted in little change. He needed to learn what tactics to avoid.

He contacted several people whom Fred Ross had mentored, among them Dolores Huerta, a divorced mother of three children and an activist. She was described

Dolores Huerta participating in the grape boycott in California.

as "outspoken even when her views differed from those of male leaders. This dynamic, intense, fast-talking, and alert woman was assertive and aggressive."[3] She lived in Stockton, California, and helped Frank Ross start the Stockton chapter of the CSO, which "battled segregation and police brutality, led voter registration drives, pushed for improved public services and fought to enact new legislation."[4]

EARLY STRIKES BY MEXICAN AMERICANS

AWOC's and Chávez's efforts were not the first for Mexican American farmworkers. In 1903, "more than 1,000 Mexican and Japanese workers, toiling in the beet fields...struck for wages and better conditions. They organized the Sugar Beet and Farm Laborers Union of Oxnard [California]. Included among strikebreakers were Japanese from San Francisco," wrote Sam Kushner in *The Long Road to Delano*. "In a shooting fracas, a Mexican striker was killed and four others injured. Following the traditional pattern in the farm communities, police arrested all of the union officials. A representative of the California State Federation of Labor, AFL, was sent to the scene and aided in the defense. Finally, the unionists were released and the strike was won."[6]

Huerta cofounded the Agricultural Workers Association, which in 1960 became the Agricultural Workers Organizing Committee (AWOC), composed of black, Chicano (a Spanish term for Mexicano), Filipino, and Anglo workers. AWOC was a branch of the American Federation of Labor-Congress of Industrial Organization (AFL-CIO), a national federation of trade unions. AFL-CIO is an umbrella organization with dozens of associated unions representing workers.

In 1962, Dolores Huerta joined César, and along with Helen they developed their strategy. "Instead of staying in one community and trying to organize workers against a background of repeated failures over the past forty or fifty years, we decided to visit most of the communities in the San Joaquin Valley," Chávez reported. "We visited something like seventy-eight communities, including small rural communities and large labor camps. At each of these places we went after those people who were already convinced—those workers who wanted to fight and struggle to form a union."[5]

THE NFWA FLAG

As journalist Ed Fuente explains, "César's brother, Richard, and his cousin, Manuel, begin working on flag designs, borrowing the symbol of the eagle from the Aztecs, the indigenous people so many Mexican Americans identify with. On a brown paper wrapper, as the legend goes, the first initial designs

Farmworkers Organize

The NFWA flag is displayed during a meeting to organize a strike against vineyard owners in California.

of an eagle with squared-off wings were created, and chosen ... Andrew Zermeño, a graphic-artist friend of the family, interpreted the wings as an inverted pyramid." César selected the colors red, black, and white. "According to UFW lore [César]

(continued on the next page)

César Chávez: Fighting for Migrant Farmworkers

(continued from the previous page)

picked black to represent the darkness of the farmworker's plight and the white to mean hope, all set against a red that signified the sacrifice expected from union workers," Fuente continues. "The eagle's head faces to the right, looking to the future. Under wings that mirror the architecture of Mesoamerican temples, the image is anchored in the past, and the base replaces talons, giving it a peaceful stability."

The flag graphic could easily be reproduced by commercial printers or created by trained and amateur artists because the graphic "lines were so definite and simple." The symbol "was worn on hats protecting marchers from the sun, used on picket signs, or stenciled on homemade serapes."[7]

Uniting Farmworkers

César, Helen, Dolores, and volunteers traveled from town to town in the central valleys of California and tirelessly built an organization that they hoped would be effective in campaigns. Chávez, Huerta, and Gilbert Padilla, a former member of the CSO and close friend of César's, founded the National Farm Workers Association (NFWA). They called themselves an association because in the past unions and strikes had failed. As a result, farmworkers shied away from joining a union. Chávez also emphasized that NFWA would be a collective effort to improve the lives of Mexican Americans.

NFWA held a convention in an old theater on September 30, 1962, and delegates representing farmworkers formally established their association. Delegates elected César Chávez president and Dolores Huerta and Gilbert Padilla vice presidents. During the convention, a flag symbolizing the NFWA was unfurled.

Joining Filipino Workers

By 1965, the NFWA had a membership of 1,700 workers who used the slogan *"viva la causa"* (live the cause). Although it was small, NFWA was well enough established that Filipino AWOC leader Larry Itliong asked for Chávez's help. The Filipino workers had walked off their jobs in the Delano-area vineyards. Chávez was not sure how much assistance his small group could provide, but he agreed to join the AWOC strike.

Philip Vera Cruz was another leader of AWOC. He described what life had been like in the past for Filipinos in Delano:

> *Filipinos were blamed for taking the Anglos' jobs. Racist growers and politicians picked on the Filipino minority as a[n] easy target for discrimination and attack. Filipinos were harassed and driven from their jobs. But the sad thing was they didn't have anywhere else to go. They were pushed to the wall and the whole town was against them. The police made false arrests and threw them in jail. In certain cases the courts imposed excessive fines. Those poor unwanted people risked their lives even just to go and buy their groceries. In those race riots staged in their camps, some were hurt and one was shot in bed…Filipinos banded*

together even tighter than did other farm workers...Exploited and oppressed by labor contractors, they sought refuge in union organization, which by the middle of the 20th century was primarily expressed through membership in the AFL-CIO Agricultural Workers Organizing Committee."[8]

On September 16, 1965, a day that commemorates Mexican independence from the US, Mexican American migrant workers joined the Filipino farmworkers union in a strike against owners of Delano, California, vineyards. As farmworkers left vineyards, they shouted *"¡Huelga, Huelga!"* (Strike! Strike!). Workers were striking for better pay and working and living conditions. At the time, wages for picking grapes was about $1.25 or less per hour, plus 10 cents for every basket picked.[9] Workers lived in slovenly shacks and while picking grapes, they had no

Farmworkers Organize

Under a massive banner, InterHarvest representative Armando Ruiz speaks during the United Farm Workers (UFW) convention in 1975.

clean drinking utensils—they had to share a beer can for drinking. There were no toilet facilities.

César Chávez, along with labor leader Dolores Huerta and the Filipino strikers, planned to lead a protest march. Before they put their plan into action, US senators visited California to hold hearings designed to extend labor rights to farmworkers. Unlike other laborers, farmworkers (as well as domestics) were not protected under the National Labor Relations Act (NLRA) of 1935. The act guarantees the right of employees in industry, commerce, business, and so forth to organize and bargain collectively with their employers. Such employees have the right to discuss unionizing with coworkers, engage in strikes and pickets and other activities. Employees are also protected from certain types of employer and union misconduct.[10]

In March 1966, Senator Robert F. Kennedy, brother of assassinated president John F. Kennedy, was one of the senators attending a hearing in Delano. A crowd gathered in the Delano High School auditorium for the hearing. Senator Kennedy, who was roundly cheered, told the audience that he would push hard for a bill to give all farmworkers the chance to bargain collectively with their employers.

During the event, one witness was a sheriff who was "trying to rebut strikers' charges of police harassment," according to a *New York Herald-Tribune* report. The sheriff "testified that he arrested 44 pickets one day because they were 'potential troublemakers.' Sen. Kennedy appeared stunned. 'How can you arrest someone if they haven't violated the law?' he asked. 'Well, I heard some of the people out in the fields (non-strikers) were going to cut up the pickets,' the sheriff answered. 'So I arrested the pickets…for unlawful assembly."[11] The senator pointed out that the sheriff was violating the US Constitution.

Unfortunately, the hearings did not bring about changes in the NLRA. Growers applied political pressure on Republicans in Washington, who defeated the attempt to amend the NLRA. However, with Senator Kennedy's appearance and news coverage of impoverished workers and conditions in fields, national attention focused on the plight of migratory workers.

4

Pressing On

After the Senate hearings in March 1966, the group of Mexican American and Filipino strikers began a protest march, which was like a religious pilgrimage. They planned to travel more than 300 miles (482 km) from Delano to the state capitol building in Sacramento, California. At the capitol the strikers expected to call nationwide attention to the deplorable conditions of farmworkers and to encourage workers to join the NFWA.

The marchers carried bedrolls, chanted, and waved American flags and the NFWA flag on poles. Some marchers held posters of Our Lady of Guadalupe, the patron saint of Mexico. They sang "Nosotros Venceremos"—the civil rights anthem "We Shall Overcome." The religious element discouraged those who opposed the protest from physically attacking the marchers.

During the month-long march, Chávez suffered from chronic back pain. Like other walkers he also developed blisters on the soles of his feet. But by using a cane he was able to press on. Chávez wanted to demonstrate his belief in sacrifice. He would endure the pain as a penance, self-punishment for la causa (the cause). Besides that, he was stubborn and did not want to give up and look like a failure.

Pressing On

Grape strikers on a 300-mile (482 km) trek from Delano to Sacramento, California, in 1966, carrying their banners high.

A Merger

During and after the pilgrimage from Delano to Sacramento, Chávez faced increasing pressure to become part of the labor movement. The Filipino leaders urged him to merge with their union under the AFL-CIO umbrella. Chávez adamantly opposed traditional unions in part because they did not espouse social justice. But he had to be practical because the NFWA needed funds. They were also threatened by fierce competition: the Teamsters Union was organizing workers in the vineyards, and the union was known for corruption and violence.

A STRIKER REMEMBERS

On the fiftieth anniversary of the grape pickers strike, musician Agustin Lira, who had been a migrant worker alongside with his family members, was interviewed by Andrea Castillo of the *Fresno Bee*. She reported that Lira expected he would spend his life working in the fields. But he read about the NFWA and their mission. The group needed volunteers, so he and Luis Valdez founded El Teatro Campesino, a theater group that performed "on picket lines, at meetings and rallies."

On the picket lines, strikers met brutal resistance. "It was a continual struggle," Lira said. "In the beginning, people would be injured and beaten. Later on, people got killed. Luis Valdez was picked up and slammed around by members of the Teamsters union, who were brought in by the growers to oppose us."

He continued: "During the early marches, if we didn't march with religious figures they would have shot us down in the streets. The FBI infiltrated UFW from beginning ... [and also] conducted widespread surveillance and disruption efforts of activist leaders, including Chávez and Martin Luther King Jr."[1]

Chávez finally agreed to a merger. In September 1966, the United Farm Workers Organizing Committee (UFWOC) was born, simply referred to as the UFW. "One immediate benefit was badly needed financial help," wrote author Miriam Pawel. "The AFL-CIO provided an immediate $10,000-a-month subsidy."[2] The funds helped the UFW continue the strike over the next four years and to press on for Mexican American rights.

In 1967, Chávez decided to try a different tactic. He launched a nationwide boycott of California table grapes. He organized a network of activists in cities across the United States and Toronto, Canada. Activists marched, carrying signs urging people to boycott grapes, and talked to consumers about their cause.

The UFW was not free of internal conflicts, however. Resentments cropped up when some members were paid—though small amounts—and others received no compensation except thanks for their work. Some members were disgruntled about the emphasis on sacrifice. There were arguments over trustworthiness. If people in the organization showed signs of disloyalty, Chávez ordered them to leave.

Loyalty was an issue with Teatro Campesino—the farmworkers' theatre troupe that had accompanied strikers on the pilgrimage. The group was popular with the public and within the union. Valdez took the troupe on tours, publicizing the farmworker plight. As Teatro gained acclaim, Valdez planned a fifteen-city tour, but Chávez demanded that the group break up and pitch in to work on a campaign against a major grower. To Valdez, disbanding seemed counterproductive. He believed his group was helping wherever they performed. When the UFW board voted against the Teatro tour, Valdez quit the union. However, he still supported the UFW, insisting that his dramatic efforts called attention to the union and that he would continue in a way that he knew best.

Valdez was not the only person to have a falling out with Chávez. The grape boycott was not making much progress in terms of its effect on growers. Strikers were getting discouraged and some wanted more direct action to scare vintners, such as burning down growers' grape-storage buildings and sabotaging refrigerated rail cars transporting grapes. But the disgruntled strikers did not change Chávez's mind.

Forty Acres and a Fast

Before the UFW formed, Chávez had a vision for helping poor farmworkers. He wanted to create a service center where workers could find assistance for daily needs like health care, banking, legal aid, child care, automobile repairs, and reasonably priced gas and groceries. Chávez

A mariachi band performs under a United Farm Workers (formerly known as the National Farm Workers Association) banner at a rally in Salinas, California, in 1975.

ordered the farmworker association to buy forty acres of barren land in Delano, California. Appropriately enough, the land was named "Forty Acres," and the first building was a gas station with a small office and a storeroom, which became a room for Catholic mass. A multipurpose hall, health clinic, and retirement village for Filipino American farmworkers were also on the property.

In February 1968, Chávez announced at a union meeting that he was going to begin a fast, and he did not know how long it would be. His purpose, he said, was not to fast as a strike tactic, but instead to rededicate his movement to nonviolence. Chávez said his fast would be spiritual, like a prayer, and he would stay at Forty Acres.

The UFW members were taken by surprise. Some were worried about Chávez's health and were against the fast. Filipino board member Larry Itliong was upset about the entire idea. He thought the union would suffer if Chávez was not actively at the helm. Still others were in awe and compared Chávez to a saint.

No matter what people thought or said, César Chávez had made a decision. He would proceed with his fast. His brother Richard and several volunteers set up a small area for César in the gas station and supplied a cot, electricity, and heat for the windowless room. "Within days, Forty Acres became a shrine," Pawel wrote.[3] No one was allowed to drive onto the property, but a priest came daily for mass and numerous farmworkers came to visit. Some camped on the grassland outside the Forty Acres building.

Chávez's fast went on for days and then weeks. He became so weak that he was close to death. After twenty-five days, on March 10, 1968, he broke his fast. Senator Robert Kennedy had flown to Los Angeles, and then by helicopter to Delano, to be at Chávez's side. After he deplaned, he was accompanied by UFW's Dolores Huerta and a legislative aide. "Kennedy wore on his left lapel a version of the UFW's black and red Aztec eagle button," the *Los Angeles Times* reported. At Delano, "Kennedy…[joined] an estimated 6,000-10,000 persons, mostly Chicano, or Mexican American, migrant workers, gathered to hold a 'Mass of Thanksgiving' at Memorial Park for César E. Chávez."[4]

Chávez was too weak to stand and was carried to a flatbed truck where he sat between his mother and Kennedy. With help, Chávez had prepared some remarks, which an aide read. To reaffirm the UFW's commitment to nonviolence and to symbolize the spiritual nature of his fast, he asked that the crowd break bread (as in Christian communion). Aides passed around loaves of bread, and individuals took portions for the ceremony.

> "I think that César Chávez is very influential, but I think also what in the last analysis is the answer is that we pass the laws that will remedy the injustices."

Senator Kennedy Speaks

Afterward Kennedy addressed the crowd, mindful that he was not only supporting the farmworkers but was also engaged in a primary campaign for president of the United States:

> *I think [farmworkers] are frustrated and I think they're terribly disturbed by the fact that they haven't*

César Chávez: Fighting for Migrant Farmworkers

In March 1968, Senator Robert Kennedy breaks bread with Chávez as Chávez ends a fast in support of nonviolence in the strike against grape growers.

had more success and that the federal government in Washington has not been helpful to them and that the state has not been helpful to them, and this is not only true here, but elsewhere in the country, so that there is this frustration and there is apt to be this explosion.

I think that César Chávez is very influential, but I think also what in the last analysis is the answer is that we pass the laws that will remedy the injustices. That's what we should do, that's what those of us in Washington should do.[5]

While Kennedy was in Delano he met an owner of a small vineyard. "In the presence of the press and many farmworkers, Kennedy explained to the grower that it was not the union that he had to fear but the big growers, who constituted the major problem both for the farmworkers and the small growers," Kushner wrote. "Throughout the following years, Kennedy reportedly did much to support the strike, including backing the boycott. And his wife Ethel became involved in fund-raisers for the farmworkers and in other activity to support their cause."[6]

KERRY KENNEDY REMEMBERS

In 2015, Senator Robert Kennedy's daughter Kerry wrote about her father, explaining how the senator and Chávez, in spite of their differences in upbringing, "shared a deep bond." As she explained:

> They recognized in one another a fierce commitment to justice and an unshakable belief in the individual's ability to bring it about. This common commitment first brought my father to Delano in 1966 for hearings about injustices grape strikers endured. He came back two years later to be with César on March 10, 1968, as he ended a 25-day fast reaffirming the United Farm Workers' commitment to nonviolence. After breaking bread with César, my father said, "You are winning a special kind of citizenship: No one is doing it for you—you are winning it yourselves—and therefore no one can ever take it away." That was the heart of César's vision: empowering Latino- and Filipino-American farmworkers to demand that they be recognized as human beings. But it was a vision for all Americans, a vision that should continue to guide us today as we struggle to build a society that affords everyone a decent life.[7]

Three months after his appearance in Delano, Senator Kennedy was campaigning in Los Angeles and addressed supporters at the Ambassador Hotel. He shared a platform with Dolores Huerta and spoke to an audience of primarily Mexican Americans and African Americans. After his speech, he left through a corridor to a side exit, planning to meet reporters for a news conference. Before he could leave, he was shot multiple times by an assassin named Sirhan Sirhan. Kennedy died the following day, June 5, 1968. It was five years after his brother President John Kennedy had been assassinated and only two months after Martin Luther King Jr. had been shot and killed.

5
No Rest for Strikers

After Chávez was back on the job, he continued his active leadership of the UFW strikes and boycotts of grape growers. In 1969, Chávez organized another march, this time through the Coachella and Imperial Valleys of California to the US-Mexican border. Chávez wanted to obtain contracts from vintners and also to lead a protest against the growers who hired scabs—that is, people who took strikers' jobs. Chávez was focusing on undocumented immigrants from Mexico who were strikebreakers.

It was a contentious issue. The UFW's crusade, which was called the Illegals Campaign, was under the leadership of Manuel Chávez, César's cousin. Manuel was a gambler and a troublemaker who had spent some time in prison. He often led physical attacks against undocumented immigrants from Mexico, who were referred to by the racist term "wetbacks." The label stems from the many immigrants who swam or rafted across the Rio Grande River between the US and Mexican border to enter the United States illegally.

Although Manuel was a rabble-rouser, César loved him and always defended him. César also supported the Illegals Campaign and its "wet line" established at the US-Mexican border. There UFW members under

US Border Patrol agents drive along the US-Mexican border, looking for undocumented immigrants who may have crossed into the United States.

Manuel's leadership set up camp to capture and turn over undocumented immigrants to the US Immigration and Naturalization Service, the agency now called the Customs and Border Protection. In Chávez's view, deporting the immigrants was necessary because owners of vineyards deliberately encouraged Mexican workers to come into the United States illegally to replace UFW members.

> "I was given no choice but to call the Border Patrol and turn in my own people."

César Chávez: Fighting for Migrant Farmworkers

One woman, Jessie de La Cruz, who had worked in the fields for decades and had been a striker since 1965, had this to say about an incident with nonunion workers:

I was called upon to do something I never thought I would do, but I had no choice. As the strike grew and we gained strength, the growers started hiring scabs in order to work the fields. Most of these people were recent arrivals from Mexico and had no idea of all the struggles and hardships we had to go through in order to improve working conditions. I was given no choice but to call the Border Patrol and turn in my own people. It was an awful feeling, like I had betrayed my heritage and the home country of my parents. I tried to convince myself this was for the benefit of everyone, yet I could not help but cry. But as the year moved along and we started making contracts I became more determined than ever. [1]

Chávez and the UFW were not alone in opposing illegal immigration, of course. Author David G. Gutiérrez, who grew up in the Mexican American community of East Los Angeles, pointed out that there was an "almost comical love/hate relationship between US born Mexican Americans and more recent immigrants from Mexico. In my own family, for example, I often heard my relatives complain about lenient immigration policies…My family griped about many different aspects of immigration, but their most common complaints were that Mexican wetbacks or illegals, as they often called them, were displacing Mexican American workers, depressing wages, and undermining union-organizing efforts."[2]

Another author, Ruben Navarrette Jr., wrote a similar account:

> *For those of us born and raised in the San Joaquin Valley, the nuances of the tale of Chávez and the UFW are not so easily pushed aside. In my own Mexican American family, for example, there has never been consensus over Chávez and the movement he inspired and led. A generation ago, there were heated arguments at my grandparents' dinner table. My grandfather, born in the Mexican state of Chihuahua...spent his entire life as a farm worker, a packing house foreman and, finally, as a small farmer himself. He knew hard work, injustice and racism. He had an unyielding sense of right and wrong. He also had an outright distaste for—and distrust of— Chávez and the UFW...[M]y grandfather was far more sympathetic to farmers who put people to work in the fields than to those he regarded as agitators trying to lure people out of the fields for a strike.*
>
> *His rigid view clashed with that of his five sons, who were...swept up in a push for radical social change. For them, the UFW was bravely standing up for dignity, justice and righteousness.*[3]

Competing with Teamsters for Contracts

Throughout the years of the grape boycott, UFW picketed supermarkets in major US cities such as Boston, Chicago, Detroit, New York, and Philadelphia, and Montreal and Toronto in Canada. By July 1970, numerous growers had agreed to sign a contract with the UFW. The agreement "raised the workers' wages to $1.80 per hour. In addition, the growers would donate 10 cents per hour to the Robert Kennedy Health and Welfare Fund. The contract provided for all hiring to be through the union hiring hall and for the protection of workers from certain pesticides. The victory in Delano now meant that almost 85 percent of all table grape growers in California were under a union contract," reported Richard Griswold del Castillo.[4]

Yet, there were problems for farmworkers in other areas—mainly in the lettuce fields of Salinas Valley, California. The UFW had been trying to organize farmworkers there, but growers refused to recognize the UFW. Instead companies sided with the Teamsters Union. "The terms of the contract between the Teamsters and the lettuce growers called for an annual increase of two cents per hour over the $1.25 which workers [then earned]," according to a report in the *Harvard Crimson*. Pickets at Harvard had successfully protested the use of non-union lettuce in the university's dining halls. However, the Crimson reported:

> *No provisions were made for health care, housing, or educational facilities. Nothing in the contract mentioned the growers' practice of spraying fields with DDT while pickers were working, which had caused much blindness and skin disease. The farmworkers were not eager to accept this pact. Although the Teamsters threatened to fire workers who refused to join the union, only about ten per cent of the approximately 700 farmworkers in the Salinas Valley had signed the pact by August 8.*[5]

The UFW had hoped and once believed that the Teamsters were an ally in the farmworker movement. But the Teamsters often used devious and sometimes violent methods to accomplish their goal of representing farmworkers. Physical attacks on those who opposed the Teamsters were common.

When the UFW asked lettuce growers to allow workers to hold elections to determine which union would represent them, growers announced that they had signed with the Teamsters. But the workers had not been consulted, and Chávez only heard of the decision when it was reported on the radio. That soon prompted action. UFW workers left the fields and in August 1970 began strikes against three dozen companies. Thousands of workers picketed lettuce fields.

In September, a county judge issued an order prohibiting all UFW strike activity. The judge ruled that California law forbids strikes when the dispute is between two unions. Chávez called off the strike and instead ordered UFW to boycott growers and consumers of non-union lettuce. But that led to Chávez's arrest for defying the court order. He served twenty days in jail, with people outside holding vigils. Chávez was released the day before Christmas 1970.

"The boycotts, work stoppages and marches, later dubbed the 'Salad Bowl' strike, took place in waves between Aug. 23, 1970, and March 25, 1971," according to the Farmworkers Forum. "The strike consisted of repeated pickets, protests, and walk-outs and ultimately involved nearly 10,000 farm laborers—making it one of the largest labor actions in the country's history up to that point." On March 26, 1971, "the Teamsters gave up their contracts with growers and signed a three-year pact with the UFW, agreeing to stop organizing farmworkers and honor the UFW's right to do so."[6]

Moving UFW Headquarters

After this success, Chávez moved UFW headquarters from Delano to Keene, California, where a donor had helped him purchase 100 acres of land. Volunteers constructed buildings that included a meeting hall, an educational center, housing, a health clinic, and a small home for the Chávez family. Chávez "wanted a name [for the headquarters] that combined religious imagery and peace," wrote Miriam Pawel. "He christened the retreat Nuestra Senora de la Reina de La Paz. Our Lady Queen of Peace. The compound quickly became known as La Paz."[7]

La Paz became a community of fellow union members and volunteers who worked for social justice. The full-time staff "were 'paid' $5 a week (doubled to $10 a week in the late '70s) plus room and board. La Paz offered them respite from tough struggles in the fields and cities," according to a UFW press release. "Roughly 250 people, mostly volunteer staff and their families, lived and labored at La Paz at any one time from the 1970s on."[8]

Pesticide Poisoning

Farmworkers in the 1940s and 1950s knew little about the dangers of pesticide use. There were some instances of workers mishandling chemicals and causing injury to themselves and others. But Rachel Carson's book *Silent Spring* published in 1962 brought public attention to the

The beautiful site called "La Paz" in Keene, California, is now the National Chávez Center and the burial site of union organizer César Chávez.

dangers of the common pesticide dichlorodiphenyltrichloroethane, better known as DDT. However, her book emphasized the effects of this pesticide on the environment rather than on humans.

In the late 1960s, the UFW began to focus on the use of DDT, which caused harmful physical effects on farmworkers. When César Chávez testified before a US Senate committee in 1969 about labor problems, he told the senators about the dangers to farmworkers exposed to pesticides. He called them "economic poisons" because growers used chemicals to increase production and their income. He said:

> *An especially serious problem in agricultural employment is the concerted refusal of growers even to discuss their use of economic poisons or pesticides. There are signs that several members of Congress are becoming increasingly aware of the dangers posed by economic poisons to human life and to wildlife, to the air we breathe and the water we drink. Senator Gaylord Nelson of Wisconsin is to be congratulated for proposing a federal ban on DDT. For us the problem is before all else one of worker health and safety. It is aggravated in California by the refusal of county agricultural commissioners to disclose their records of pesticide application and by state court injunctions against such public disclosure.[9]*

His testimony along with that of UFW lawyers, members of the union, doctors, chemists and others increased public awareness about the dangers of pesticides. The Senate hearings prompted hundreds of news articles about pesticide poisoning, raising public concern about the issue. Eventually regulations at the state and federal levels outlawed the use of DDT except under state and federal emergency conditions, such as spraying the chemical to eradicate moths destroying fir trees in a national forest.

However, pesticide poisoning continued. Farm worker Juan Rios sprayed pesticides on grapes at a winery in Washington State. Interviewed by Rebecca Clarren for a 2003 issue of *The Nation*, he sat "beneath a portrait of Cesar Chavez and a Mexican flag…[at] the United Farm Workers union local, and said 'I remember the first time I worked with the pesticides, I was wearing a full mask while we were spraying, but my nose, it wouldn't stop bleeding. I was worried.'" According to the article, "Rios is not alone. As many as 300,000 farmworkers are injured annually by pesticides, and of these as many as 1,000 die."[10]

Organophosphates

When DDT was outlawed in 1972, more dangerous organophosphates were used to control agricultural pests. The Occupational Safety and Health Act states:

> *Pesticides, herbicides and fungicides used in the agricultural industry have increasingly become recognized as a particular source of hazard to large numbers of farmworkers. One of the major classifications of agricultural chemicals—the organophosphates—has a chemical similarity to commonly used agents of chemical and biological warfare, and exposure, depending on degree, causes*

headache, fever, nausea, convulsions, long-term psychological effects, or death.[11]

These chemicals also have "been shown to cause neuromuscular impairment varying from mild muscular weakness to serious deterioration of strength and hand-to-eye coordination," the report pointed out. [12]

On October 21, 1972, the Federal Environmental Pesticides Control Act (FIFRA) was enacted. The act governs the registration, distribution, sale, and use of pesticides in the United States. According to the law, "Facilities that handle pesticides must adopt workplace practices designed to reduce or eliminate exposure to pesticides and must establish procedures for responding to exposure-related emergencies. FIFRA prohibits registration of pesticides that generally pose unreasonable risks to people, including agricultural workers, or the environment."[13]

The passage of FIFRA and the ban on DDT appeared to be a victory for farmworkers. But legislation in the state of Arizona was presenting another type of problem for the UFW. And Chávez resolved to take action.

6
"Lett-us" Strike Again

In the spring of 1972, Chávez learned that Arizona lawmakers had passed a bill banning the UFW from the state. Chávez decided to visit Arizona governor Jack Williams to try to persuade him not to sign the bill. But the governor refused and the law went into effect on May 11, 1972.

UFW members and supporters were so incensed with the state's ban that they took part in a campaign to recall Governor Williams, using the cry "Si se puede!" (Yes, we can!) as a slogan—one that Barack Obama borrowed years later for his presidential campaign. Although "the union gathered more than enough signatures" for the recall, the state's "attorney general disqualified" it, declaring some signatures were improper. But the ruling was overturned by a federal court years later.[1]

After the law took effect, César Chávez announced at a UFW rally at the Capitol building in Phoenix that he would begin a water-only fast. According to the union newspaper *El Malcriado*, published June 9, 1972:

> [Chávez] said that he was fasting against fear—the fear of the Union which drove the Farm Bureau and growers to seek this legislation; the fear of the Arizona legislature and the Governor in the face of

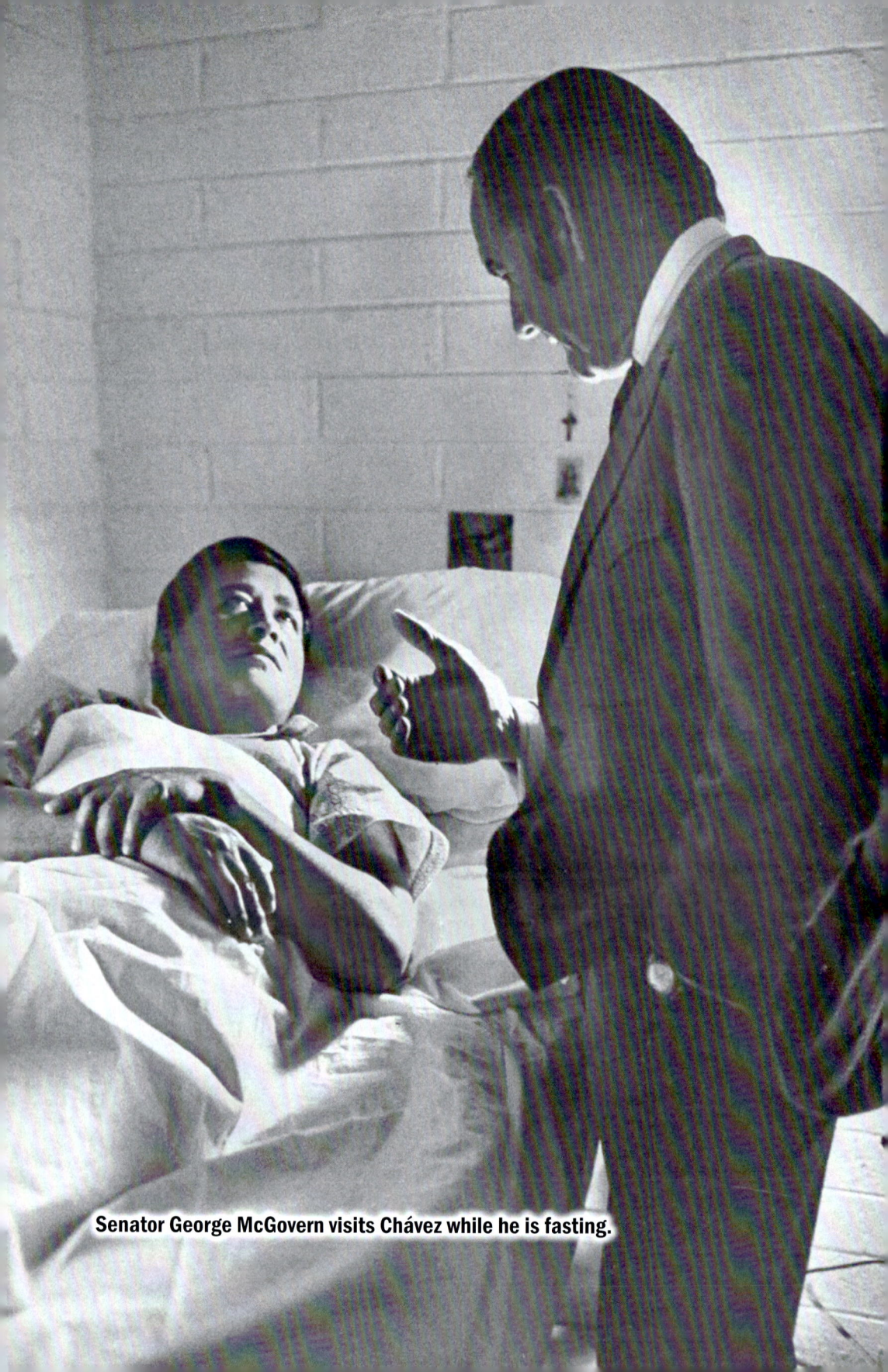

Senator George McGovern visits Chávez while he is fasting.

the massive economic and political power of the Farm Bureau which led them to pass and sign the bill; and the fear that Arizona farmworkers have of the power which others hold over their lives...In an exclusive interview with EL MALCRIADO, César said: "The fast was started to create the spirit of social justice in Arizona and to try by our efforts through the fast and our sacrifices to erase the fears that the growers and the Republican legislators and the Republican Governor have of the Union. The fast is to try to reach the hearts of those men, so that they will understand that we too have rights and we're not here to destroy, because we are not destroyers, we're builders.[2]

While Chávez continued his fast, supporters in major cities gathered pledges to boycott growers and consumers of non-union lettuce. There were protest marches, weekend fasts, vigils, religious observances, masses, press conferences, and other events to demonstrate solidarity with Chávez. His fast, however, was endangering his life. He became so weak that he could not get out of bed, and doctors insisted that he begin taking nourishment. After twenty-four days, he ended his fast and was taken to a hospital to be treated for heart problems and vitamin deficiencies.

"I am weak in my body but I feel very strong in my spirits."

Chávez prepared a statement that was read to his followers. In part, he said:

> *I am weak in my body but I feel very strong in my spirit...In fact, what is a few days without food in comparison to the daily pain of our brothers and sisters who do backbreaking work in the fields under inhuman conditions and without hope of ever breaking their cycle of poverty and misery. What a terrible irony it is that the very people who harvest the food we eat do not have enough food for their own children...Our opponents in the agricultural industry are very powerful...But we have another kind of power that comes from the justice of our cause. So long as we...persist in non-violence and work to spread the message of our struggle, then millions of people around the world will respond from their hearts, will support our efforts...and in the end we will overcome.*[3]

An Audience with the Pope

In September 1974, Chávez traveled to Europe to meet with union leaders in London and other European cities to request assistance in the UFW grape boycott. While in Europe, Chávez, with a group of religious leaders, went to the Vatican in Rome, Italy, for an audience with Pope Paul VI. The pope met privately with the group on September 24, 1974, saying in part:

> *Our welcome goes this morning to César Chávez whom we are happy to receive as a loyal son of the Catholic Church and as a distinguished leader and representative of the Mexican American community in the United States. We wish to tell you of the real joy that is ours to be informed of the fidelity of the people of your culture and origin, our beloved sons*

Chávez, with a group of religious leaders, went to the Vatican in Rome, Italy, for an audience with Pope Paul VI, shown here.

and daughters…We know, in particular, of your sustained effort to apply the principles of Christian social teaching, and that in striving to do so you have faithfully worked together with the Bishops of your country and with the support of their authoritative representatives.[4]

Labor Legislation

The UFW strikes in the 1970s paved the way for the passage of the California Agricultural Labor Relations Act of 1975. The law dramatically altered how farm laborers in California were treated by their employers. The legislation guaranteed that California farmworkers had the right to vote by secret ballot for union representation. Governor Jerry Brown signed the measure in June and it took effect in September 1975. The law protects the right of agricultural workers to designate "representatives of their own choosing, to negotiate the terms and conditions of their employment, and to be free from the interference, restraint, or coercion of employers of labor, or their agents." The act also provides for collective-bargaining rights for agricultural employees.[5]

Farm owners were adamantly opposed to the legislation and worked to overturn the California ALRA. Agricultural lobbyists urged California legislature to cut off appropriations for the ALRA board, who enforced the law. By February 1976, the board had no funds with which to operate. So Chávez ordered the UFW to collect signatures for a petition, known as Proposition 14 (or Prop 14), which would make the labor law part of the California Constitution, thereby insuring annual funding for the ALRA board.

A TRAGEDY

Farmworkers were and often still are transported to fields and orchards by refurbished buses or vans crowded beyond capacity. Some of these vehicles have crashed and killed many workers. One tragic case occurred on January 15, 1974. Farmworkers in an unsafe school bus were being transported to Blythe, California, when the driver, who was speeding, lost control of the vehicle and plunged into an unguarded irrigation ditch. The *Los Angeles Times* and other media outlets covered the tragedy, but *El Malcriado*, the official voice of the UFW, published personal accounts and photos of the accident. "According to survivors, the bus went off the road because it was travelling too fast to make the sharp right-hand turn at the corner of [an intersection]. It plunged headfirst into the drainage ditch and fell onto its side," the newspaper reported. "The force of the impact in the ditch tore the seats loose from the floor of the bus, trapping the victims in what one survivor described as a 'prison' of seats."

Nineteen workers were killed and twenty-eight others were injured. A second bus arrived shortly after the crash, and workers jumped out to help the victims. But the foreman on the second vehicle ordered the driver to take the workers on to the Blythe lettuce fields and tend to the weeding (with the short-handled hoe). The foreman warned workers not to talk about the accident.[6]

Prop 14 would go "a step further than federal labor law," Chávez told Tom Hayden of *Rolling Stone* in a 1976 interview. "It very plainly states that the law is there to protect the rights of workers to organize. But we also added another clause which says that not only should the law 'protect' but also…encourage the rights of workers to organization. If we can get Proposition 14 passed and enforced very vigorously, I would not be at all surprised if we organized 100,000 workers in California in the next 18 months."[7]

However, because of the petition drive, agricultural businesses dropped their opposition. In their view, if the legislature restored funding for the ALRA board, then there would be little justification for passage of Prop 14. Still, Chávez refused to withdraw. Farm owners then engaged in another tactic. They widely publicized their argument that the proposition, if passed, would permit union organizers to invade their property. It was a matter of property rights—a potent argument. The proposition was defeated by a two to one margin.

Chaos in the Ranks

After the Prop 14 initiative failed, some UFW members became discouraged and began to grumble about the future of the union and were critical of Chávez. As former UFW volunteer and economics professor Michael Yates explained at the time:

> *The UFW is not well administered. During my stay I observed that research projects were generally superficial and haphazard. Records were either not*

kept or strewn about, stuffed in boxes, stored at random in basements and cubbyholes. Negotiators often took no notes of their meetings, or took notes so poor as to be useless. Repeatedly, negotiators in one part of the state were unaware of agreements reached elsewhere; generally speaking, communications throughout the union were woefully slipshod…

Those who criticize him are perceived as threats to himself and to the union (indeed, in his mind there is little separation between the two). Dedicated, hardworking men and women, essential to the smooth functioning of the union, were accused, on little or no evidence, of being radicals, spies for the employers, troublemakers, complainers. They were told to leave the union, or were pressured into quitting.

Yates noted that the reason for the UFW purges was because Chávez was in complete control and he did "not want the UFW to become just another trade union…The UFW must be a social movement, encompassing wider goals than bargaining collectively for higher wages and better working conditions." Chávez wanted to develop a social movement that would embrace farmworkers who were being steadily replaced by mechanization.[8]

In pursuit of his goal for a social movement—that is, a farmworkers movement—César Chávez consulted with Charles Dederich, a man who supported the UFW and had become his friend. Dederich had founded a drug rehabilitation program, which by 1977 had become a cult-like community called Synanon with various sites in California. Synanon's home base was in the foothills of the Sierra Nevada Mountains.

Synanon, a drug rehabilitation center, was founded by Charles Dederich, who supported César Chávez and the UFW.

At first, Synanon was for illegal drug addicts and alcoholics who were subjected to relentless group attacks to force them to own up to their addiction, go "cold turkey," and begin to live without drugs. Later, people were attracted to Synanon's communal living, an alternative lifestyle that became widely popular beginning in the 1950s. Chávez was impressed with Dederich's ability to solicit funds for his communes and provide help for UFW members.

Chávez was most captivated by "the Synanon Game," a procedure in which people sat in a circle and vented their frustrations and complaints about one another in a confrontational way. In some cases, accusations were not based on fact and were simply a tactic to get participants to deal with problems. As one participant explained: "In this setting, eight or ten members would sit in a circle and talk, cajole, confront, scream and break through barriers with others in that setting. The most heinous charges, and the most miniscule, were handled with the same sledgehammer approach. People learned to say their piece and defend themselves, or counter-attack."[9]

When Chávez visited and witnessed the Game, he decided to use the method for UFW members in order to purge the union of those he deemed were troublemakers. At a meeting in 1977 at the La Paz headquarters, Chávez used the Game to attack several volunteers working with the UFW. Some were kicked out or left the union. Chávez continued to use the Game to test the loyalty of UFW members and assure that he maintained absolute control.

7

Internal and External Scuffles

In the early 1980s, Chávez and the UFW were "major players in California agriculture and politics," according to the Center for Immigration Studies. "But the writing was on the wall for a major loss of UFW power. Several long-time supporters left the UFW and accused Chávez of losing touch with newly-arrived farmworkers." Although most people acknowledged that Chávez was a charismatic leader, the UFW had numerous problems. One example: "union-run health and pension plans sometimes failed to pay doctors and workers in a timely fashion, prompting dissatisfaction with the UFW among members."[1]

When the union engaged in strikes, they were broken by labor contractors, who were employed by ranch or farm owners. The contractors hired crew leaders who supervised, directed, or controlled agricultural workers. To disrupt strikes, contractors simply hired scabs—usually undocumented workers. In short, the contractors made sure that crews were not pro-union.

In addition, there were more purges of farmworker leaders who disagreed with Chávez. To protest, one group of expelled farmworkers began a fast that lasted for eight days. They publicly aired complaints that the union was not operating democratically and that Chávez was acting like a dictator.

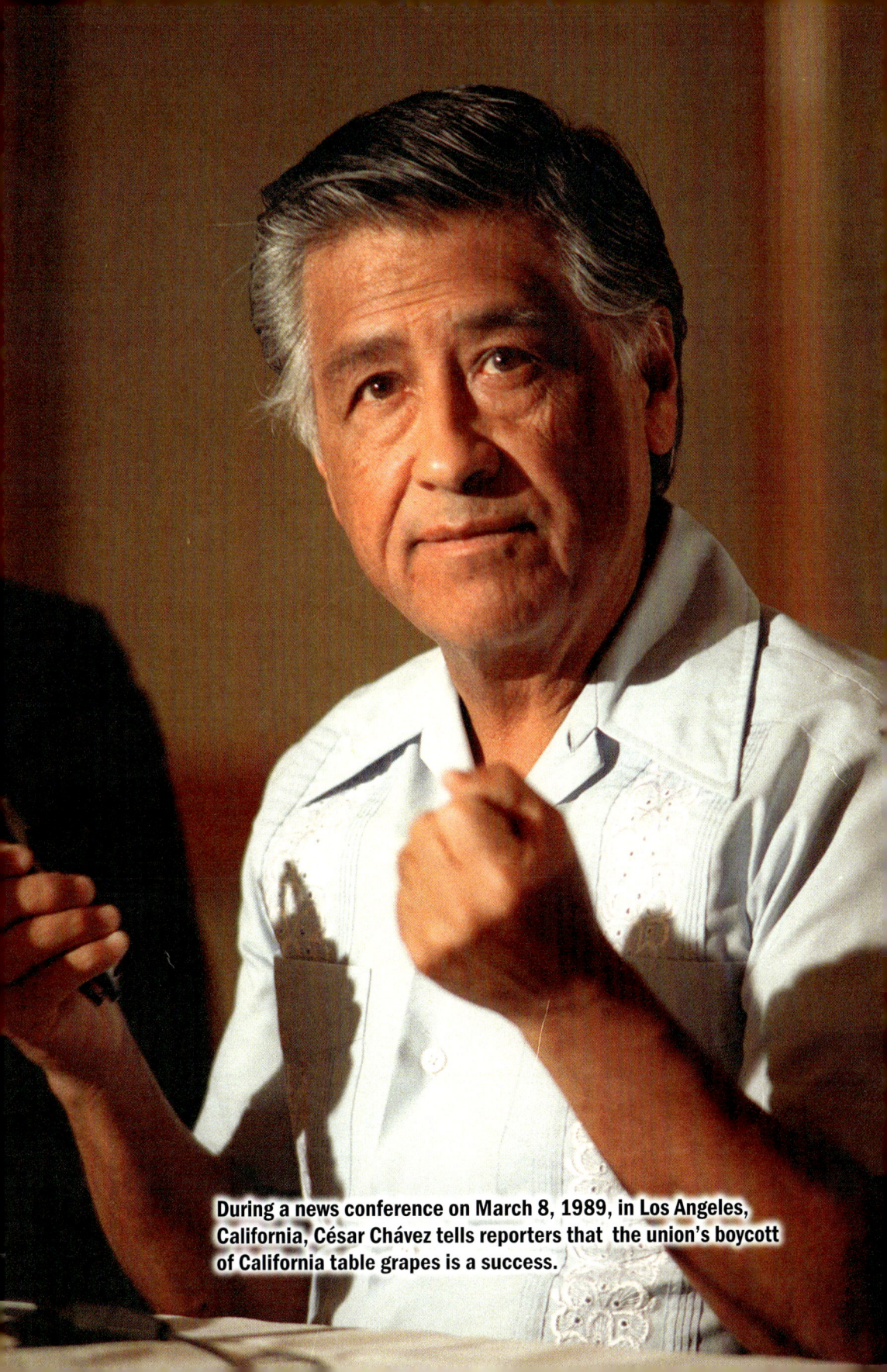

During a news conference on March 8, 1989, in Los Angeles, California, César Chávez tells reporters that the union's boycott of California table grapes is a success.

César Chávez: Fighting for Migrant Farmworkers

> "Everybody served at the pleasure of César Chávez and the executive board."

"In the UFW there was no way for worker opinion to be expressed," said Frank Bardacke, author of *Trampling Out the Vintage: César Chávez and the Two Souls of the United Farm Workers*. As a former teacher and radical political activist, Bardacke worked in the Salinas Valley for six seasons and then taught English as a second language at an adult school for many years. He explained in a 2012 interview with *The Nation*:

> *Everybody served at the pleasure of César Chávez and the executive board. If you didn't like what the union was doing, you didn't put up a fight. You quit…There were lots of conflicts [in the UFW]…There was no way for local farmworkers to be elected to the UFW staff. The UFW had field offices staffed by people appointed by the people above them, so they were responsible not to the workers but to the people above them…The staff kind of looked down on farm work. But for a Mexican immigrant, the fields, especially in the mid-1970s, made for a great success story—they were making fabulous wages compared to Mexico. The fields were not something to get out of. The fields where a place where people built successful lives.*[2]

Regardless of conflicts, worker dissatisfaction, and loss of contracts, Chávez and Dolores Huerta soldiered on. Chávez once more ordered boycotts of table grapes. He focused on the dangers of pesticides, spending little time on organizing workers.

Internal and External Scuffles

PESTICIDE PROTECTION

When consumers were poisoned in the summer of 1985 after eating watermelons grown in California, "investigators discovered that several growers in the state had used illegal pesticides on their watermelon acreage," the UFW reported. "The union attributed the high rate of birth defects and cancer deaths among farm worker children to pesticide use. In response, the legislature in 1986 expanded California's food testing program and made more stringent the assessments measuring the health

(continued on the next page)

Notice	Aviso
Migrant and Seasonal Agricultural Worker Protection Act	**Ley de Protección de Trabajadores Migrantes y Temporales en la Agricultura**
This federal law requires agricultural employers, agricultural associations, farm labor contractors and their employees to observe certain labor standards when employing migrant and seasonal farmworkers unless specific exemptions apply. Further, farm labor contractors are required to register with the U.S. Department of Labor.	Esta ley federal exige que los patrones agrícolas, las asociaciones agrícolas, los contratistas de mano de obra agrícola (o troqueros), y sus empleados cumplan con ciertas normas laborales cuando ocupan a los trabajadores migrantes y temporales en la agricultura, a menos que se apliquen excepciones específicas. Los contratistas, o troqueros, tienen además la obligación de registrarse con el Departamento del Trabajo.
Migrant and Seasonal Farmworkers Have These Rights	**Los Trabajadores Migrantes y Temporales en la Agricultura Tienen los Derechos Siguientes**
• To receive accurate information about wages and working conditions for the prospective employment • To receive this information in writing and in English, Spanish or other languages, as appropriate • To have the terms of the working arrangement upheld • To have farm labor contractors show proof of registration at the time of recruitment	• Recibir detalles exactos sobre el salario y las condiciones de trabajo del empleo futuro • Recibir estos datos por escrito en inglés, en español, o en otro idioma que sea apropiado • Cumplimiento de todas las condiciones de trabajo como fueron presentadas cuando se les hizo la oferta de trabajo • Al ser reclutados para un trabajo, ver una prueba de que el contratista se haya registrado con el Departamento del Trabajo

This notice describes, in both English and Spanish, a federal law to protect farmworkers and their families from illegal pesticides.

> (continued from the previous page)
>
> effects of pesticide residues, particularly on young people."[3]
>
> Nationally, the Environmental Protection Agency finally initiated a Worker Protection Act in 1992, and it was revised in 2015 (to take effect in 2017). The revised EPA regulations require annual training of farmworkers and pesticide handlers, signs that pesticides have been used in fields, basic safety information for workers posted in a central location, decontamination supplies, and prompt transportation to a medical facility if a worker is poisoned. All regulations are posted on EPA's website.[4]

As for Huerta, she was adamant about organizing for *la causa*. In fact, she was often criticized within and outside the union for being away from her husband and children for long periods of time to recruit union members. Huerta's "schedule was filled with speaking engagements, fund raising, and publicizing the renewed boycotts of the 1980s. Appearing before state and congressional committees, she passionately testified on a variety of issues including pesticide use, the health problems of field workers, Hispanic issues, and immigration policy," according to scholar Margaret Rose. Rose noted that in 1988, Huerta was clubbed with a baton by a police officer while protesting peacefully against then-presidential candidate George Bush in San Francisco. She had to undergo emergency surgery, in which her spleen was removed, and stayed at the hospital for a long period of time. Huerta was determined to fight for farmworkers' rights, despite suffering physical and psychological harm. Due to her grave injury, Rose wrote, "the San Francisco police department changed its rules dealing with crowd control and police discipline. In 1991, she was awarded a record financial settlement as a consequence of the personal injury."[5]

New Federal Law

The UFW hoped that the federal Migrant and Seasonal Agricultural Worker Protection Act (AWPA), which passed in 1983 and was amended in 1986, would support their cause. The AWPA included these requirements:

> [Agricultural] employers must disclose terms of employment at the time of recruitment and comply with those terms; employers, when using farm labor contractors ("FLCs" or "crewleaders") to recruit, supervise or transport farmworkers, must confirm that the FLCs are registered with and licensed by the US Department of Labor; providers of housing to farmworkers must meet local and federal housing standards; and transporters of farmworkers must use vehicles that meet basic federal safety standards and are insured. The Act does not apply to owners of small farms.[6]

Despite the AWPA, agricultural employers often ignored the rules. Housing for workers, for example, was (and still is) often substandard. Overcrowded and unsafe vans and buses carried farm laborers to fields and orchards, risking accidents. At some work sites there were no toilets or hand-washing facilities. And workers often had to provide their own drinking water.

Fast for Life

In 1986, under Chávez's leadership, the UFW tried to intensify its boycott of grapes by demanding a ban on five of the most dangerous pesticides and making an agreement with growers to test for poisonous residues on the fruit. But the union did not have the resources to send volunteers around the country to picket in front of stores. So Chávez ordered the UFW to conduct a direct-mail campaign, with flyers warning consumers that grapes contained traces of poisonous pesticides. He also commissioned a short video titled *The Wrath of Grapes*, showing young children who, the film asserted, had developed cancer or bore physical defects due to pesticide poisoning. The film also depicted brutal attacks on UFW members. The union sent the video free of charge to any group requesting it. Although most people watching the film were appalled at scenes of abuses against farmworkers and the horrors of pesticide poisoning, consumers did not provide the support for the grape boycott as they had in the 1960s.

To call attention to the health hazards farmworkers faced, Chávez announced that he would undertake another public fast as an act of atonement for what he perceived as his failure to properly protect farmers from the harmful effects of pesticides. He went to Forty Acres in Delano, the original UFW headquarters, where he began his fast on July 18, 1988. "The national media exhibited a kind of fatigue about Chávez's fast until members of the Robert Kennedy family visited, and joined one of the daily picket lines protesting grape sales at a Delano grocery store,"

A Delano, California, policeman confronts Chávez during a union march for farmworker rights in the 1960s.

wrote Pat Hoffman, a board member of the National Farm Worker Ministry, which supported Chávez.[7]

> "Today I pass on the fast for life to hundreds of concerned men and women throughout North America and the world."

On August 18, Chávez ended his thirty-six day fast with a mass held in a tent outside the retirement building. In an article for *The Christian Century* magazine, Hoffman reported:

> *More than 7,000 supporters attended the mass, and at least 80 percent of those were farm workers… When Chávez was brought into the tent that Sunday morning carried by two of his sons, the thousands who had come to be with him stayed seated in silence, at Chávez's request…Chávez's, oldest son, Fernando… read his father's brief statement, which concluded: "Today I pass on the fast for life to hundreds of concerned men and women throughout North America and the world who have offered to share the suffering.*
>
> *They will help carry the burden by continuing the fast in front of their local supermarkets. The fast will go on in hundreds of distant places and it will multiply among thousands and then millions of caring people until every poisoned grape is off the supermarket shelves."*[8]

César Chávez's wish would not come to pass.

8
A Downward Trend and Tributes

Unfortunately for the UFW, Chávez's fast did not produce any noteworthy changes for the union or the boycott. Frustrated, Chávez found scapegoats; he blamed the failures on farmworkers and union leaders, claiming they were disloyal or guilty of theft or fraud. As on previous occasions when Chávez felt betrayed, he purged numerous members, some of them long-time friends and supporters. Those purged or who quit included lawyers, advisors, fund-raisers, and priests. Even his loyal friend and former UFW vice president Gilbert Padilla resigned. Philip Vera Cruz also left the union. "Gradually La Paz became a ghost town," Pawel wrote.[1]

At the end of the 1980s into the next decade, tensions continued between Chávez and UFW members. Chávez wanted to engage in boycotts and a farmworkers movement sustained by volunteers, while UFW members wanted to build a business-like union with paid leadership. When the 1980s ended, the UFW had "fewer than 15,000 members, and by the early 1990s the union had only a handful of contracts, which covered around 5,000 workers," according to Daniel Rothenberg, author of *With These Hands: The Hidden World of Migrant Farmworkers Today*.[2]

César Chávez ponders an interviewer's question during an April 14, 1993, visit to Dartmouth College in Hanover, New Hampshire.

A Downward Trend and Tributes

Chávez continued to engage in protests against the use of pesticides on table grapes. He toured colleges to speak about the UFW's grape boycott. And in 1992, he traveled abroad to visit major buyers of grapes and discuss the poisonous effects of pesticides.

In 1993, Chávez and the UFW were in court in Yuma, Arizona. A major lettuce and vegetable grower, Bruce Church, Inc. (BCI), had sued the union for damages resulting from a California boycott in the 1980s. The company began legal action in 1984 in Arizona because the company had a lot of acreage in the state and Arizona's farm labor relations law prohibited secondary boycotts. In 1993, the company renewed its lawsuit.

BCI claimed that the UFW had made libelous, or false, statements about the corporation, which caused supermarkets, McDonald's, and other large companies to quit buying Church lettuce. The trial in Yuma, Arizona, lasted for two days and recessed on April 22, 1993. When Chávez left the court he returned to the home of Doña Maria Hau, a friend and former farm worker. Chávez along with other UFW leaders and staff had been staying at the Hau home.

PERSONAL LOSSES

Beside the downward spiral of the UFW, Chávez faced personal sorrows. His mother died in 1991 at the age of ninety-nine. At her funeral Chávez credited his mother with teaching him about nonviolence. The following year, Fred Ross died. In a eulogy for Ross, Chávez said that his mentor had changed his life.

WHAT'S A SECONDARY BOYCOTT?

The National Labor Relations Board explains: "The NLRA protects the right to strike or picket a primary employer—an employer with whom a union has a labor dispute. But it also seeks to keep neutral employers from being dragged into the fray. Thus, it is unlawful for a union to coerce a neutral employer to force it to cease doing business with a primary employer."[3]

Reportedly Chávez ate dinner, held a meeting about the trial, and went to bed around 10 p.m. The next morning, when Chávez did not appear as he usually did around 6 a.m, staff members checked on him and found him unresponsive. He had apparently died in his sleep. A physician confirmed his death on April 23, 1993.

On April 29, tens of thousands attended a funeral for Chávez. They came from across the United States to pay respects. According to news reports, it was the largest funeral for a labor leader in US history. His oldest son, Fernando Chávez, presented a eulogy, in which he said in part:

> My father chose to live a life of voluntary poverty and yet I believe that his legacy will be rich. His legacy to our family, his legacy to all of you here and to the whole country is a legacy of nonviolence. A legacy

A Downward Trend and Tributes

An estimated 25,000 mourners accompany the pine casket of farm labor union leader César Chávez through farmlands to his funeral mass on April 29, 1993.

in the tradition and spirit of Gandhi, Martin Luther King, and Bobby Kennedy.

My dad's life has proven to me that his nonviolent struggle for the rights of farmworkers was a true manifestation of his faith in God and his practice of the teachings of the Gospel.

Some people might say that my father was a "famous man" or that he was a "VIP." Perhaps he was. But for all of us who knew him, including all of you here, I can attest to the fact that he was never, ever too busy to give his complete attention and interest to each and every person with whom he spoke. Be that person a field worker, a store clerk, a student, a grieving parent, or a complete stranger. He was that kind of man.[4]

Tributes

After César Chávez's death, tributes to "that kind of man" came from hundreds of people across the United States and other countries. His family and friends established the César E. Chávez Foundation to educate Americans, especially young people, about the life and work of this labor and civil rights leader. On the first anniversary of Chávez's death, Arturo Rodriguez, who became president of the union, led a 343-mile (552-km) march following the route of the 1960s pilgrimage from Delano to Sacramento.

On August 8, 1994, then president Bill Clinton posthumously awarded Chávez the Medal of Freedom, America's highest civilian honor. His wife, Helen, accepted the medal during a White House ceremony in which Clinton declared that Chávez had "faced formidable, often violent opposition with dignity and nonviolence. And he was victorious. César Chávez left our world better than he found it, and his legacy inspires us still."[5]

> **"César Chávez left our world better than he found it."**

Throughout the decade and into the 2000s tributes continued. Schools in California were given his name. Parks in San Jose, Berkeley, Sacramento, and Long Beach, California, were named after him. At the University of Arizona, there is a César E. Chávez Building. Streets in California, Colorado, Arizona, Texas, and Midwestern states bear the Chávez name. Chávez birthday celebrations

A Downward Trend and Tributes

are held in several states. In various US cities, Chávez is honored at Mexican heritage days. The César Chávez Foundation hosts annual César Chávez Legacy Awards honoring individuals who demonstrate their commitment to community and advocacy.

Chávez's life has been covered in diverse media. For example, a 1996 PBS four-part series called *Chicano! History of the Mexican-American Civil Rights Movement* includes Chávez's campaigns for Mexican American equal rights in the 1960s and 1970s. Films about Chávez's life are currently available on DVDs and on YouTube.

The state of California recognized the legacy of César Chávez when the governor at the time, Gray Davis, signed a 2000 law to honor Chávez's birthday each year on March 31. Also established was a César Chávez day of learning, when the state's public schools teach about César Chávez and his union.

In 2003, the US Postal Service issued a postage stamp with Chávez's portrait. The National Chávez Center was opened in 2004 at the UFW headquarters in Keene, California. In 2006, then California governor Arnold Schwarzenegger and First Lady Maria Shriver instated César Chávez into the California Hall of Fame. The National Park Service registered Nuestra Senora Reina de La Paz ranch to the National Register of Historic Places in 2011.

As all the tributes and honors show, César Chávez left a lasting legacy in buildings, statues, diverse media, and celebratory remembrances. But perhaps the most important legacy is the fact that this religious, dedicated, stubborn, rebel stuck to his cause and inspired countless people to advocate with him for farmworker justice.

César Chávez: Fighting for Migrant Farmworkers

A garland is placed on a statue of César Chávez at Fresno State University in California during annual ceremonies honoring the legacy of the labor-rights leader.

A Downward Trend and Tributes

He and the UFW, striving against numerous obstacles, achieved unprecedented gains for farmworkers. And despite membership losses in the 1990s, the UFW climbed back up, its membership slowly rising again. To this day, members along with the public honor Chávez as one of the most important Mexican American labor figures in US history.

Conclusion

Over the years, the UFW under the leadership of César Chávez, revealed for the US public and government officials what life was truly like for agricultural farmworkers—both undocumented and citizen laborers. The picture was not pretty. But slowly, using strikes and boycotts, the UFW was able to obtain agreements between workers and growers to allow collective bargaining—that is, negotiations to establish wages, working conditions, and other labor-related issues agreed upon by the employer and the union representing laborers.

The first UFW contracts required "rest periods, toilets in the fields, clean drinking water, hand washing facilities, banning discrimination in employment and sexual harassment of women workers, requiring protective clothing against pesticide exposure, prohibiting pesticide straying while workers are in the fields and outlawing DDT and other dangerous pesticides (years before the US Environmental Protection Agency acted)," according to the Chávez Foundation.[1] Other benefits that the UFW achieved include a health and welfare fund; a pension plan for retired farmworkers; contracts providing for profit sharing and parental leave; a law banning the short-handled hoe; and diverse rights for immigrants.

Even more important is the fact that César Chávez emphasized that workers' skin color, language, culture, and lack of educational opportunities were used to deprive them of basic human rights. He demonstrated that nonviolent strategies used by Mohandas Gandhi and Dr. Martin Luther King Jr. could also be effective for farmworkers.

Conclusion

Modern-day agricultural laborers have continued some of those strategies. Although not a union per se, the Coalition of Immokalee Workers (CIW)—which includes many people of Mexican heritage, African Americans, and others of color—is an example of farmworkers organizing for their rights and better pay through nonviolent means. The coalition was initiated in 1993 by laborers in Florida tomato fields, where one-third of all US tomatoes are grown. They held marches and engaged in fasts and work stoppages in order to increase their wages.

CIW made news when they investigated and assisted in the prosecution of numerous field bosses across the southeastern United States who literally enslaved Mexican workers—holding them in chains, locking them in shacks and trucks, and beating them to force them to work in agricultural fields. Because of the coalition's efforts, over 1,200 workers were freed and the federal Trafficking Victims Protection Act of 2000 was passed.

In 2010–2011, CIW also began a Fair Foods Campaign to convince major supermarkets and fast food companies to pay one cent more per pound for tomatoes to support a wage increase for workers in tomato fields. Tomato growers and major companies such as Walmart, Taco Bell, McDonald's, Burger King, Whole Foods, Subway, Chipotle, Trader Joes, and others have since signed Fair Food agreements.

Despite the CIW and Chávez models for organizing farmworkers, questions remain in regard to the treatment and exploitation of laborers in US agricultural fields and orchards. Will thousands of undocumented field workers be deported in the coming years? What will happen when the number of farmworkers diminishes? How will increasing mechanization on farms affect workers?

When, if ever, will UFW and other farm laborers have the same protections under the Fair Labor Standards Act as non-farmworkers?

Answers to those questions, if known, would likely fill another book. In the meantime, consumers can support and advocate for farmworkers through such programs as the UFW Foundation, Farmworkers Ministry, the CIW, Farmworker Justice, the Center for Farmworker Families (in California), and similar organizations. As César Chávez himself put it: "The fight is never about grapes or lettuce. It is always about people."[2]

CHRONOLOGY

1927 César Estrada Chávez is born on March 31, in Yuma, Arizona.

1937 Chávez's parents lose the family homestead amidst the Great Depression.

1946 César Chávez enlists in the US Navy.

1948 Chávez is discharged from the military and marries Helen Fabela.

1949 César and Helen's first child, Fernando, is born.

1952 Chávez meets Roman Catholic priest Father Donald McDonnell and community organizer Fred Ross.

1959 He joins and organizes National Farm Worker's Association (NFWA).

1962 Chávez leaves NFWA and begins organizing farmworkers in the fields.

1965 NFWA joins Filipino workers in a strike against grape growers in Delano, California.

1966 Chávez leads a protest march from Delano to Sacramento, California.

1967 NFWA merges with AFL-CIO affiliated Filipino union, forming the United Farm Workers Organizing Committee, or the UFW.

1968 Chávez begins a twenty-five-day fast to emphasize nonviolent protest for farmworker justice.

1969 Chávez organizes a march from Imperial Valley to the US-Mexican border to organize strike against grape growers.

César Chávez: Fighting for Migrant Farmworkers

1971 UFW headquarters moves to Keene, California, and is named La Paz.

1972 Chávez fasts for twenty-four days to protest Arizona's antiunion laws.

1973 Teamsters Union takes over representation of farm laborers and UFW membership declines.

1975 California Agricultural Labor Relations Act passes and gives farmworkers the right to vote for union representation.

1976 Chávez uses cult-like Synanon's confrontational methods to purge disloyal UFW members.

1983 Federal Migrant and Seasonal Agricultural Worker Protection Act passes.

1986 A UFW video *Wrath of Grapes* shows alleged victims of pesticide poisoning.

1988 Chávez fasts for thirty-six days to protest pesticides.

1992 Chávez travels abroad to discuss poisonous effects of agricultural pesticides with major buyers.

1993 While staying at a friend's home in Arizona, Chávez dies in his sleep April 23; thousands attend his funeral.

Chapter Notes

Chapter 1: Overcoming Hard Times

1. Richard Griswold del Castillo, *"Burning with a Patient Fire:" The Legacy of César Estrada Chávez* (San Diego, CA: San Diego State University, 2001), http://chavez.cde.ca.gov/ModelCurriculum/Teachers/Lessons/Resources/Biographies/High_School_Bio.pdf.

2. Fredrick John Dalton, *The Moral Vision of César Chávez* (Maryknoll, NY: Orbis Books, 2003), p. 33.

3. Miriam Pawel, *The Crusades of César Chávez: A Biography* (New York, NY: Bloomsbury Press, 2014), p. 9.

4. Studs Terkel, *Hard Times: An Oral History of the Great Depression* (New York, NY: New Press paperback, 2005), p. 53, http://www.rialto.k12.ca.us/rhs/planetwhited/AP%20PDF%20Docs/Unit%2011/Depression/Chávez4.pdf.

5. United Farm Workers, "The Story of César Chávez," http://www.ufw.org/_page.php?menu=research&inc=history/07.html.

6. Griswold del Castillo, *"Burning with a Patient Fire."*

7. Jacques E. Levy and César Chávez, *César Chávez: Autobiography of La Causa* (Minneapolis, MN: University of Minnesota Press, 2007), p. 84.

8. Miriam Pawel, *The Crusades of César Chávez: A Biography*, p. 90.

9. Jacques E. Levy and César Chávez, *César Chávez: Autobiography of La Causa*, p. 84.

10. Miriam Pawel, *The Crusades of César Chávez: A Biography*, p. 21.
11. Jacques E. Levy and César Chávez, *César Chávez: Autobiography of La Causa*, p. 50.

Chapter 2: Community Organizing

1. Peter Dreier, "The Grapes of Roth," *Huffington Post*, February 2, 2013, http://www.huffingtonpost.com/peter-dreier/fred-ross-presidential-medal-of-freedom_b_2757989.html.
2. Gabriel Thompson, "Ross, Fred," *Teaching a People's History: Zinn Education Project*, http://zinnedproject.org/materials/ross-fred.
3. Miriam Pawel, *The Crusades of César Chávez: A Biography* (New York, NY: Bloomsbury Press, 2014), p. 83.
4. Richard Griswold del Castillo, *"Burning with a Patient Fire:" The Legacy of César Estrada Chávez* (San Diego, CA: San Diego State University, 2001), http://chavez.cde.ca.gov/ModelCurriculum/Teachers/Lessons/Resources/Biographies/High_School_Bio.pdf.
5. Records in the California State Archives for the Study of Labor History, 2015, pp. 21–22, http://archives.cdn.sos.ca.gov/pdf/ref-guide-labor.pdf.
6. Eyder Peralta, "It Came Up in the Debate: Here Are 3 Things to Know About 'Operation Wetback,'" NPR, November 11, 2015, http://www.npr.org/sections/thetwo-way/2015/11/11/455613993/it-came-up-in-the-debate-here-are-3-things-to-know-about-operation-wetback.
7. Bracero History Archive, 2016, http://braceroarchive.org/about.

8. Student Non Violent Coordinating Committee, "César Chávez Talks About Organizing and the History of the NFWA," *UC San Diego Library*, https://libraries.ucsd.edu/farmworkermovement/essays/essays/MillerArchive/009%20César %20Chávez%20Talks%20About%20Organizing.pdf.

9. Griswold del Castillo, *"Burning with a Patient Fire."*

Chapter 3: Farmworkers Organize

1. Student Non Violent Coordinating Committee, "César Chávez Talks about Organizing and The History of the NFWA," *UC San Diego Library*, https://libraries.ucsd.edu/farmworkermovement/essays/essays/MillerArchive/009%20César %20Chávez%20Talks%20About%20Organizing.pdf.

2. César Chávez, "Address to United Farm Workers of America," *Commonwealth Club of California*, November 9, 1984, http://www.Chávezfoundation.org/_cms.php.

3. Richard Griswold del Castillo, *"Burning with a Patient Fire:" The Legacy of César Estrada Chávez* (San Diego, CA: San Diego State University, 2001), http://chavez.cde.ca.gov/ModelCurriculum/Teachers/Lessons/Resources/Biographies/High_School_Bio.pdf.

4. National Women's History Museum, https://www.nwhm.org/education-resources/biography/biographies/dolores-fernandez-huerta.

5. César Chávez, "A Union in the Community," 1969, https://libraries.ucsd.edu/farmworkermovement/essays/essays/MillerArchive/029%20A%20Union%20In%20The%20Community.pdf.

6. Sam Kushner, *The Long Road to Delano*, (New York, NY: International Publishers, 1975), https://libraries.ucsd.edu/farmworkermovement/essays/essays/CORRECTED%20KUSHNER%20ROAD%20TO%20DELANO.pdf.

7. Ed Fuentes, "How One Flag Went from Representing Farmworkers to Flying for the Entire Latino Community," *takepart*, April 2, 2014, http://www.takepart.com/article/2014/04/02/cultural-history-ufw-flag.

8. Kushner, *The Long Road to Delano*.

9. United Farm Workers, "UFW History," http://www.ufw.org/_page.php?menu=research&inc=history/03.html.

10. "Employee Rights Under the National Labor Relations Act," *US Department of Labor*, https://www.dol.gov/olms/regs/compliance/employeerightsposter11x17_final.pdf.

11. Dick Meister, "Support from Robert Kennedy," *New York Herald-Tribune*, 1966, https://libraries.ucsd.edu/farmworkermovement/ufwarchives/meister/06%20UFWMeister66-5-RFK.doc.pdf.

Chapter 4: Pressing On

1. Andrea Costillo, "Former United Farm Workers Volunteer Looks Back on 1965 Delano Grape Strike," *Fresno Bee*, September 24, 2015, http://www.fresnobee.com/news/local/article36494277.html.

2. Miriam Pawel, *The Crusades of César Chávez: A Biography* (New York, NY: Bloomsbury Press, 2014), p. 139.

Chapter Notes

3. Miriam Pawel, *The Crusades of César Chávez: A Biography*, p.161.

4. Paul Darwin Lee, "Senator Robert F. Kennedy Visits Delano 1968," *UC San Diego Library*, https://libraries.ucsd.edu/farmworkermovement/category/commentary/senator-robert-kennedy-visits-delano-1968.

5. Paul Lee, *¡Si, Se Puede! (Yes, We Can!): Bobby Kennedy Visits César Chávez-REVISED*, YouTube, August 2, 2010, https://www.youtube.com/watch?v=qQndvfZyf7w.

6. Sam Kushner, *The Long Road to Delano*, (New York, NY: International Publishers, 1975), https://libraries.ucsd.edu/farmworkermovement/essays/essays/CORRECTED%20KUSHNER%20ROAD%20TO%20DELANO.pdf.

7. Kerry Kennedy, "Kerry Kennedy: Robert F. Kennedy and César Chávez—A Friendship for the Ages," *Monterey Herald*, June 13, 2015, http://www.montereyherald.com/article/NF/20150613/NEWS/150619890.

Chapter 5: No Rest for Strikers

1. UFW, "Veterans of Historic Delano Grape Strike Mark 40th Anniversary with Two-day Reunion in Delano and La Paz," *El Malcriado*, September 17-18, 2005, http://www.ufw.org/_page.php?menu=research&inc=history/05.html.

2. David G. Gutiérrez, *Walls and Mirrors: Mexican Americans, Mexican Immigrants, and the Politics of*

Ethnicity. (Berkeley and Los Angeles, CA: University of California Press, paperback, 1995), p. 2.

3. Ruben Navarrette Jr., "Review: *The Fight In The Fields: César Chávez and the Farmworkers Movement*," *Los Angeles Times*, April 13, 1997, http://articles.latimes.com/1997-04-13/books/bk-48126_1_la-causa.

4. Richard Griswold del Castillo, "*Burning with a Patient Fire:*" *The Legacy of César Estrada Chávez* (San Diego, CA: San Diego State University, 2001), http://chavez.cde.ca.gov/ModelCurriculum/Teachers/Lessons/Resources/Biographies/High_School_Bio.pdf.

5. "Farm Workers Press Lettuce Boycott," *Harvard Crimson*, November 13, 1970, http://www.thecrimson.com/article/1970/11/13/farm-workers-press-lettuce-boycott-ppicketing.

6. Farmworkers Forum, "40 Years Later: Salinas Valley Labor Clashes Still Resonate," March 26, 2011, https://farmworkersforum.wordpress.com/2011/03/26/40-years-later-salinas-valley-labor-clashes-still-resonate.

7. Miriam Pawel, *The Crusades of César Chávez: A Biography* (New York, NY: Bloomsbury Press, 2014), p. 80.

8. UFW, "Historical Back Stories on César Chávez and La Paz," *United Farm Workers*, October 9, 2012 http://www.ufw.org/_board.php?mode=view&b_code=news_press&b_no=12746.

9. César Chávez, "Statement of César E. Chávez 1969," *UC San Diego Library*, https://libraries.ucsd.edu/farmworkermovement/essays/essays/MillerArchive/031%20Statement%20Of%20César%20E.%20Chávez.pdf.

Chapter Notes

10. Rebecca Clarren, "Fields of Poison: While Farmworkers Are Sickened by Pesticides, Industry Writes the Rules," *The Nation*, December 29, 2003, p. 23.

11. Ellen S. Greenstone, "Farmworkers in Jeopardy: OSHA, EPA, and the Pesticide Hazard," scholarship.law.berkeley.edu, September 1975, p. 72 http://scholarship.law.berkeley.edu/cgi/viewcontent.cgi?article=1099&context=elq.

12. Ellen S. Greenstone, "Farmworkers in Jeopardy: OSHA, EPA, and the Pesticide Hazard," p. 84.

13. "Federal Insecticide, Fungicide, and Rodenticide (FIFRA) and Federal Facilities," *United States Environmental Protection Agency*, https://www.epa.gov/enforcement/federal-insecticide-fungicide-and-rodenticide-act-fifra-and-federal-facilities.

Chapter 6: "Lett-us" Strike Again

1. Miriam Pawel, *The Crusades of César Chávez: A Biography* (New York, NY: Bloomsbury Press, 2014), p. 241.

2. "César Chávez Fasts in Arizona," *El Malcriado*, June 9, 1972, https://libraries.ucsd.edu/farmworkermovement/ufwarchives/elmalcriado/1972/June%209,%201972%20No%203_PDF.pdf.

3. "Statement by César Chávez at the End of His 24-Day Fast for Justice, Phoenix, Arizona," June 4, 1972, http://Chávez.cde.ca.gov/ModelCurriculum/teachers/Lessons/resources/documents/EXR1_César_E_Chávez_Statements_on_Fasts.pdf.

4. "Statement by Pope Paul VI at Private Audience for César Chávez and Party," September 25, 1974, http://Chávez.cde.ca.gov/ModelCurriculum/Teachers/Lessons/Resources/Documents/PCCCP2_Box9_21_Statement_by_Pope_Paul_VI.pdf.

5. "Labor Code Section 1140-1140.4," *Official California Legislative Information*, http://www.leginfo.ca.gov/cgi-bin/displaycode?section=lab&group=01001-02000&file=1140-1140.4.

6. "Drowned in 'Prison of Seats': 19 Lettuce Workers Die in Contractor Bus Massacre," *El Malcriado*, February 22, 1974, p. 1–2, https://libraries.ucsd.edu/farmworkermovement/ufwarchives/elmalcriado/1974/No.2%20February%2022,%201974_PDF.pdf.

7. Tom Hayden, "César Chávez and His Many-Layered Union," *Rolling Stone*, November 4, 1976, http://www.rollingstone.com/politics/news/César-Chávez-and-his-many-layered-union-19761104.

8. Michael D. Yates, "A Union Is Not a Union," *Monthly Review*, November 19, 1977, http://mrzine.monthlyreview.org/2006/yates160106.html.

9. Laura Johnston Kohl, "Peoples Temple and Synanon—Modern Communities: The Role of Women," *Alternative Considerations of Jonestown and Peoples Temple*, last modified May 20, 2014, http://jonestown.sdsu.edu/?page_id=34288.

Chapter 7: Internal and External Scuffles

1. Philip L. Martin, "Promise Unfulfilled," *Center for Immigration Studies*, January 2004, http://cis.org/Unionization-CaliforniaFarmLabor.

Chapter Notes

2. Jon Wiener, "César Chávez and the Farmworkers: What Went Wrong?" *The Nation*, January 5, 2012, https://www.thenation.com/article/César-Chávez-and-farmworkers-what-went-wrong.

3. United Farm Workers, "The Reagan Years: 1980s: UFW Protests Pesticides Use," *Oakland Museum of California*, http://picturethis.museumca.org/timeline/reagan-years-1980s/united-farm-workers/info.

4. "Quick Reference Guide to the Worker Protection Standard (WPS) as Revised in 2015," *Pesticide Resources*, http://pesticideresources.org/wps/hosted/quickrefguide.pdf.

5. Margaret E. Rose, "Dolores Huerta: Passionate Defender of La Causa," http://Chávez.cde.ca.gov/ModelCurriculum/Teachers/Lessons/Resources/Documents/Dolores_Huerta_Essay.pdf.

6. Farmworker Justice, "US Labor Law for Farmworkers," https://www.farmworkerjustice.org/advocacy-and-programs/us-labor-law-farmworkers.

7. Pat Hoffman, "César Chávez's 'Fast for Life,'" *The Christian CENTURY*, October 12, 1988, p. 895 https://libraries.ucsd.edu/farmworkermovement/essays/essays/eleven/10%20-%20CÉSAR%20CHÁVEZ%20FAST%20FOR%20LIFE.pdf.

8. Pat Hoffman, "César Chávez's 'Fast for Life,'" *The Christian CENTURY*, October 12, 1988, p. 896.

Chapter 8: A Downward Trend and Tributes

1. Miriam Pawel, *The Crusades of César Chávez: A Biography* (New York, NY: Bloomsbury Press, 2014), p. 463.

2. Daniel Rothenberg, *With These Hands: The Hidden World of Migrant Farmworkers Today*, (Berkeley and Los Angeles, CA: University of California Press), 2000, p. 261.

3. National Labor Relations Board, "Secondary Boycotts (Section 8(b)(4))," https://www.nlrb.gov/rights-we-protect/whats-law/unions/secondary-boycotts-section-8b4.

4. Fernando Chavez, "Eulogy for Cesar E. Chavez," April 29, 1993, *UC San Diego Library*, https://libraries.ucsd.edu/farmworkermovement/essays/essays/chatfield2009/20%20EULOGY%20FOR%20CESAR%20CHAVEZ%20%201993.pdf.

5. "President Clinton Presents Posthumous Medal of Freedom to César Chávez at the White House," *California Department of Education*, http://Chavez.cde.ca.gov/ResearchCenter/DocumentDisplayRC.aspx?rpg=/chdocuments/documentdisplay.jsp&doc=6212dd%3Aead754e3ce%3A-7f24&searchhit=yes.

Conclusion

1. "César Chávez Foundation, http://www.Chavezfoundation.org/_page.php?code=014001000000000.

2. César Chávez, AZ Quotes, 2016, http://www.azquotes.com/quote/53704.

GLOSSARY

activist A person who advocates for or against a cause.

adobe Sun-dried clay bricks used to build houses, especially in the southwest United States.

barrio An area of a town or city inhabited by Spanish-speaking people.

chattel A possession; sometimes used pejoratively to describe slaves.

civil disobedience Refusing to obey government demands and laws as a nonviolent protest.

coalition A group, bloc, or alliance of people with common interests.

collective bargaining A method by which a union representing its workers negotiates with an employer.

epithet A disparaging word to describe a person or group of people.

Great Depression US economic crisis from 1929 into the 1930s.

gringo Once a derogatory term, now usually simply identifies a white, English-speaking person.

labor union Workers in a trade or profession who organize to advocate for their rights and interests.

La Paz Shortened version of "Nuestra Senora de la Reina de La Paz," the name for UFW headquarters.

legacy A heritage or benefit handed down from the past.

pesticide In agriculture, a general term for a chemical that kills pests that damage vegetables and fruits.

posthumous After death.

rebel A person who opposes traditions or authorities.

scab A person who refuses to strike and takes the jobs of striking workers.

serape Shawl worn in Latin America.

vintner Winemaker.

The Wrath of Grapes A UFW video showing victims of pesticide poisoning.

Further Reading

Books

Garcia, Matt. *From the Jaws of Victory: The Triumph and Tragedy of Cesar Chavez and the Farm Worker Movement.* Berkeley and Los Angeles, CA: University of California Press, 2012.

Gay, Kathlyn. *Activism: The Ultimate Teen Guide (It Happened to Me* series). Lanham, MD: Rowman and Littlefield, 2016.

Jobin-Leeds, Greg. *When We Fight, We Win: Twenty-First Century Social Movements and the Activists That Are Transforming Our World.* New York, NY: The New Press, 2016.

Pawel, Miriam. *The Crusades of Cesar Chavez: A Biography.* New York, NY: Bloomsbury Press, 2014.

Websites

Chávez Foundation

www.Chávezfoundation.org

This website describes the history, mission, and activities of the foundation.

Farmworker Justice

www.farmworkerjustice.org/advocacy-and-programs/us-labor-law-farmworkers

The Farmworker Justice website explains the US Labor Law for Farmworkers.

Records in the California State Archives for the Study of Labor History: A Reference Guide

archives.cdn.sos.ca.gov/pdf/ref-guide-labor.pdf

This site provides information about minority labor, labor camps, housing, strikes, and labor disputes.

Films

Cesar Chavez: History Is Made One Step at a Time, 2014

This 2014 biography of Chávez is available on DVD.

Selma, 2014

A video on DVD of the civil rights leader Martin Luther King Jr. and the march from Selma, Alabama, in 1965.

Index

A
Agricultural Workers Organizing Committee (AWOC), 41, 42, 45
American Federation of Labor-Congress of Industrial Organization (AFL-CIO), 42, 46, 51, 53

B
Bardacke, Frank, 86
barrios, 20, 22, 24, 26
Blythe, CA, tragedy, 79
Bracero Program, 32–33, 34
Brown, Jerry, 78
Bruce Church, Inc. (BCI), 95

C
California Agricultural Labor Relations Act of 1975, 78
California State Federation of Labor, 41
Center for Farmworker Families, 104
César E. Chávez Foundation, 98, 102
Chávez, César Estrada
 arrest, 67
 birth, 10–11
 childhood home, 11–13
 childhood as a migrant, 13–16
 death, 96–98
 discrimination against as a child, 16–17
 fasts, 56–57, 73–76, 90–92
 forming the NWFA, 44–45
 leaving CSO, 36–39
 marriage, 18–19
 Medal of Freedom, 98
 meeting with the pope, 76–78
 military service, 18
 personal losses, 95
 tributes to, 98–101
 working for CSO, 28–32, 33–35
Chávez, Césario, 10
Chávez, Fernando, 18, 29, 92, 96
Chávez, Helen (née Fabela), 18, 20, 22, 28, 29, 35, 39, 42, 44, 98

Chávez, Juana, 10, 11, 17, 22, 38, 57, 95
Chávez, Librado, 10, 11, 12, 17, 18, 38
Chávez, Mama Tella, 11
Chávez, Manuel, 42, 62–63
Chávez, Rita, 11
civil disobedience/ "Civil Disobedience," 25
Clinton, Bill, 98
Coalition of Immokalee Workers (CIW), 103, 104
communism, 6, 7, 8, 30–31, 32
Community Service Organization (CSO), 24, 25, 26, 28–32, 33, 34, 35, 36, 38, 41, 44

D
Davis, Gray, 99
DDT, 66, 68–71, 72, 102
Dederich, Charles, 81, 83
de La Cruz, Jessie, 64
Delano, CA, 13, 18, 20, 22, 39, 45, 46, 48, 50, 51, 56, 57, 59, 60, 61, 66, 68, 90, 98

E
Eisenhower, Dwight D., 32

F
Fair Foods Campaign, 103
Farmworker Justice, 104
Farmworkers Ministry, 104
Federal Environmental Pesticides Control Act (FIFRA), 72
Forty Acres, 54–57, 90
Francis of Assisi, St., influence on Chavez, 24, 36

G
Gandhi, Mohandas, influence on Chavez, 22–24, 36, 97, 102
Great Depression, 10, 13

H
Hau, Dofla Maria, 95
Huerta, Dolores, 39–42

I
Illegals Campaign, 62
Itliong, Larry, 45, 56

K
Keene, CA, 68, 99
Kennedy, Kerry, 60
Kennedy, Robert F., 48, 49, 56, 97
  assassination, 61
  speaking at Forty Acres, 57–59

Index

King, Martin Luther, Jr., 52, 61, 102

L
Lira, Agustin, 52

M
McDonnell, Father Donald, 22–24, 26, 29
Mexican Americans
  discrimination against, 16–17, 32–33
  early strikes by, 41
  Republican opposition to, 29–30, 49, 75
Mexican Farm Labor Program, 33
Migrant and Seasonal Agricultural Worker Protection Act (AWPA), 89–90
migrant workers
  discrimination against, 16–17
  life as a, 13–17

N
National Farm Workers Association (NFWA), 44–45
  grape pickers strike, 50, 52
  joining with the Filipino AWOC, 45–49
  merging under AFL-CIO, 51–52
National Labor Relations Act (NLRA) of 1935, 48, 49, 96
NFWA flag, 42–44
Nuestra Senora de la Reina de La Paz (La Paz), 68, 83, 93, 99

O
Occupational Safety and Health Act, 71–72
"Operation Wetback," 32–33
organophosphates, 71–72

P
Padilla, Gilbert, 44, 45, 93
Paul VI, 76
Proposition 14 (Prop 14), 78–80

R
"Red Scare," 30–31
Robert Kennedy Health and Welfare Fund, 66
Rodriguez, Arturo, 98
Ross, Fred, Sr., 24–28, 29, 33, 34, 39, 41, 95
Rothenberg, Daniel, 93

S
"Salad Bowl" strike, 66–68

Sal Si Puedes ("Escape if You Can"), 20, 21
San Joaquin Valley, 16, 39, 42, 65
scabs, 62, 64, 84
secondary boycott, 96
short-handled hoe (*el cortito*), 14–15, 79, 102
"Si se puede!" (Yes, we can!), 73
State Relief Administration, 30
Sugar Beet and Farm Laborers Union of Oxnard, 41
Synanon, 81–83

T
Teamsters Union, 51, 52, 65–68
Teatro Campesino, El, 52, 53
Trafficking Victims Protection Act, 103

U
United Farm Workers Organizing Committee (UFW), 52–54
  Arizona bill banning, 73–76
  competition with Teamsters, 65–68
  dissension in, 80–83, 84–86, 93
  grape boycott, 53–54, 62, 65, 76, 86, 90, 95
  lettuce boycott, 66, 67, 75, 95, 104
  moving headquarters, 68
  opposition to illegal immigrants, 62–65

V
Valdez, Luis, 52, 53, 54
Vera Cruz, Philip, 45, 93
"viva la causa," 45

W
Worker Protection Act, 88
World War II, 18, 24, 28, 32
Wrath of Grapes, The, 90

Y
Yates, Michael, 80–81
Yuma, AZ, 10, 16, 95

Z
Zermeño, Andrew, 43